Discovering
the Promise of the
Old Testament

Discovering the Promise of the Old Testament

Michael Pennock

FRIENDSHIP in the Lord Series

AVE MARIA PRESS
NOTRE DAME, INDIANA 46556

Nihil Obstat: The Reverend Edward E. Mehok, Ph.D.
Censor Deputatus

Imprimatur: The Most Reverend Anthony M. Pilla, D.D., M.A.
Bishop of Cleveland

Given at Cleveland, Ohio on February 19, 1992.

———————————

International Standard Book Number: 0-87793-472-X

Library of Congress Catalog Card Number: 91-76778

Cover and text design by Katherine Robinson Coleman

Cover photograph view from Mount Sinai by Editorial Development Associates.

Photography: Alinari/Art Resource, 124, 139; Lawrence Boadt, C.S.P., 124 (bottom), 146, 149; Cleo Freelance Photo, 38; Gail Denham, 27, 49; Editorial Development Associates, 54-55, 142, 194; Foto Marburg/Art Resource, 148; Robert Maust, 73; Marilyn Nolt, 36, 40-41, 137, 184-185; Richard Nowitz, 8, 12, 14, 20-21, 62, 68, 72, 77, 92, 98, 107 (top), 138, 152, 156, 157, 176, 186, 196 (bottom), 199; Gene Plaisted, 106, 123, 150-151, 164, 166; Zev Radovan, 22, 50, 53, 65, 79, 81, 101, 107 (bottom), 112, 132, 155, 160, 180-181, 182, 200; Religious New Service, 33, 78, 144; Sharon Remmen, 172; Lorraine O. Schultz, 37, 60, 64, 96, 118, 122, 196 (top); Florence Sharp, 171; Skjold Photographs, 91, 111; Vada Snider, 131, 175, 178; Justin A. Soleta, 66-67; Jim West, 28, 140, 168; Jim Whitmer, 11, 205.

Printed and bound in the United States of America.

To my students past and present.

Contents

chapter 1
Introducing the Old Testament

Every word of God is unalloyed,
a shield to those who take refuge in him.

— Proverbs 30:5

A distinguished scholar was a lifelong student of the bible. In his seventy-seventh year, just a month before his death, he read through the entire Old Testament in three weeks. When his daughter asked him what he was reading, he replied, "News!"

News usually refers to recent events and happenings that are notable in some way. Although the Old Testament contains the stories of events and people of centuries ago, it contains many insights that are important for us today. There are many reasons why we should read the first part of the Bible.

■ *The Old Testament is a major part of the most-read and most important book of all time.* It gave rise to some of our common expressions:

"Am I my brother's keeper?" (cf. Genesis 4:9)
"feet...of clay" (cf. Daniel 2:34)
"four corners of the earth" (cf. Isaiah 11:12)
"holier than thou" (cf. Isaiah 65:5)
"a land flowing with milk and honey" (cf. Exodus 3:8)
"there is nothing new under the sun" (cf. Ecclesiastes 1:9)
"escaped by the skin of my teeth" (Job 19:20)

■ *It contains nuggets of wisdom that helped our ancestors live their lives. We can learn from these insights as well.* Consider, for example, the wisdom of these sayings from the Book of Proverbs:

"A flood of words is never without fault;
whoever controls the lips is wise" (10:19).
"Whoever loves discipline, loves knowledge,
stupid are those who hate correction" (12:1).
"Wine is reckless, liquor rowdy;
unwise is anyone whom it seduces" (20:1).

■ *It is one of the major foundations of Western civilization.* It contains the most complete written record we possess of an ancient people. This record has significantly influenced every aspect of Western civilization: our social structures, our legal system, our ordinary religious life. It helps us understand how our society was formed.

By studying our roots, we might better understand how we should be moving in the future. For example, we live in perilous times in which nations stockpile weapons that can obliterate humanity. The Old Testament repeatedly reminds us that only justice and mercy can bring us true, permanent peace.

> Yahweh...said, "Apply the law fairly, and show faithful love and compassion toward one another" (Zec 7:9).

■ *It contains God's revelation.*   For countless millions of people — Christians, Jews, and Moslems — the Bible records God's self-communication to us, his children.

— The Old Testament contains the truth of God's promises to the Chosen People and through them to all people. God creates, forgives, blesses, and loves us, and God is faithful forever.

— It reveals our true identity as God's special creatures, God's children created out of love and called to love. Our own personal stories as individuals and as human communities are reflected in the many Old Testament stories. The Bible unmasks us, showing both our good and bad sides.

— It records the experiences of our ancestors in the faith. Jews, Moslems, and Christians all look to Abraham as the father of their faiths. The Second Vatican Council recognizes the Christian debt to the Jews for their scriptures:

> For the Church of Christ acknowledges that, according to the mystery of God's saving design, the beginnings of her faith and her election are already found among the patriarchs, Moses, and the prophets....
>
> The Church, therefore, cannot forget that she received the revelation of the Old Testament through the people with whom God in his inexpressible mercy deigned to establish the Ancient Covenant. Nor can she forget that she draws sustenance from the root of that good olive tree onto which have been grafted the wild olive branches of the Gentiles (*Declaration on the Relationship of the Church to Non-Christian Religions*, No. 4).

— We can better understand the story of Jesus by studying and reflecting on the story of his people, our mothers and fathers in the faith. Each Sunday we hear a reading from the Old Testament that helps to illuminate and explain the passage from the gospels.

— It reveals a living God who meets us when we read the Bible. This encounter has changed countless people through the centuries. It will change us.

This text will introduce you to the Old Testament and help you to mine its riches for yourself. Much of the information will be *news*, that is, noteworthy data on subjects you likely know little about.

Traveling through the scriptures will take some effort, but after a while you will gain confidence as you discover how it can help you live a life faithful to God's promises. God gave us the Bible to help us grow. May the Lord bless you as you begin your study of the word of God.

Old Testament Themes

Below are several themes from the Old Testament that remind us to draw close to God and others. Circle the number that describes most accurately the way you live these in your daily life (**5** represents much evidence of this in your life; **1** represents no evidence of this in your life).

Theme 1: Faith in God should direct our lives.

1   2   3   4   5

Meaning: I can't go it alone. I depend on God and need God's guidance to live my life.

Theme 2: We must recognize that God is God and we are God's creatures.

1   2   3   4   5

Meaning: I am not the center of the universe; without God I am nothing.

Theme 3: Life is a journey.

1   2   3   4   5

Meaning: I have an eternal destiny even though there are pitfalls along the way. I need the help of God and others to live a good life.

Theme 4: We must be people of prayer.

1   2   3   4   5

Meaning: God loves us and wants to be near us; we must approach God frequently in prayer.

Theme 5: We belong to each other.

1   2   3   4   5

Meaning: This is true for our own families, but also for the whole human community. We should pray with others, watch out for their needs, and reach out to them in love.

Theme 6: We must strive to imitate God's compassion.

1   2   3   4   5

Meaning: God continually forgave the Chosen People and extended love and mercy to the poor and helpless. We, too, must forgive and respond to the needs of others.

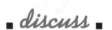

■ *discuss* ■

1. Have people in today's world forgotten about God? Explain.
2. When do people most often turn to God? Explain.

■ *journal* ■

Who is God for you? How are you most like God? Explain.

The Bible and the "Old Testament"

The English word *Bible* comes from the Greek *ta biblia* which means "the books." This gives us an accurate picture of what the Bible is — a library of inspired writings that we divide into the Old and New Testaments.

Old and New Testaments. The Catholic Bible contains seventy-three different books. Forty-six are assigned to the Old Testament and twenty-seven to the New Testament (Protestant Bibles include only thirty-nine Old Testament books). The word *testament* comes from a Latin word that translates the Hebrew word for "covenant." Thus, the various books of the Bible in one way or another tell us about God's open-ended contract of love made first with Israel through Moses (the old covenant) and with all people through Jesus (the new covenant).

Today, the Old Testament is also referred to as the Hebrew (or Jewish) scriptures. These books are primarily the sacred writings of God's special people, the Jews. The Jews traditionally divided their writings into three major categories: the *Torah* (or Law which we call the Pentateuch), the *Nebiim*

(meaning "Prophets"), and *Ketubim* (meaning "Writings"). From the first letters of each of these categories, the Jews formed the acronym *TaNaK* to refer to their holy scriptures.

There is value to using both names. First, "Old Testament" is the traditional name Christians have used throughout the centuries. The terms Old and New *Testaments* focus on continuity between the covenant God made with his people and its fulfillment through Jesus.

Some of our Jewish cousins in the faith shy away from the use of "old" to refer to their covenant with God. Some Christians have tragically interpreted "old" as meaning that God no longer cares for the Jews in light of the New Testament. A sad part of Christian history has been the crime of anti-Semitism — hatred and violence directed against the Jews in the mistaken belief that God has abandoned them. The term *Hebrew scriptures* reminds us that our Christian faith has its roots in the faith of our Jewish brothers and sisters. Their story is our story, too. We show respect and understanding for our common Jewish religious heritage when speak of the Hebrew scriptures.

Library.   The forty-six books of the Old Testament were written sometime between 1200 and 100 B.C. Some of them contain ancient fragments like Lamech's Taunt (Gn 4:23–24) and Miriam's song (Ex 15:21). These probably came from Israel's earliest days and later were incorporated in written books.

We don't know who wrote the various books in the Jewish scriptures. For example, although tradition assigned the writing of the first five books of the Bible to Moses, much of the writing of these books was anonymous.

The first stage of writing relied on *oral traditions*. For centuries tribal legends and myths, laws, stories, songs, and sacred events important to the people were passed on orally. Eventually, around the tenth century B.C., someone began to collect stories about creation and Israel's history up to the conquest of Canaan.

Other very early writings include the histories of the early kings. Next came the writings of the *prophets* and the *sages*, wise ones who taught about the ways of God and a people struggling to live God's will. Some of the prophets and sages wrote their own works. Often, however, their disciples or secretaries recorded their sayings and teachings.

Throughout the period of the Old Testament's development, many editors had a hand in collecting, combining, and changing the written materials handed down to them. Thus, most of the Old Testament books are *compilations*, the work of several writers and editors. It was standard in ancient times to borrow and rework written material and apply it to current needs and customs. This made the sacred books timely and meaningful to the current generation.

Many of the Old Testament books are a patchwork of earlier works. This accounts for the fact that some books have frequent and confusing repetitions, while others, such as the Psalms and Proverbs, are anthologies that contain the work of many people over a long period.

Writings. Most Old Testament books were written in Hebrew, but a few were written in Greek. There are just a few verses in Aramaic, the language that Jesus spoke. Ancient Old Testament books appeared first on parchment and later on papyrus scrolls. Parchment was made from skins of sheep, goats, or calves which were sewn together to make a strip ten to twenty feet long. This strip, with writing on one side, was rolled around a stick like a window shade.

Papyrus scrolls were made from a plant that was soaked and pressed into a paper-like substance. These scrolls were cumbersome to use, requiring two hands to manipulate the text. One hand unwound the scroll while the other rewound it on a second stick until the desired section of the text appeared.

In these early texts, all the words ran together without chapter and verse markings. Numbered chapters only appeared in A.D. 1228 when Stephen Langton introduced chapter headings. Numbered verses only appeared with printed Bibles, the first of which was published in 1528.

Much of what we know of these early texts comes from the Dead Sea scrolls, discovered in 1948. This archaeological find contains a scroll of the book of Isaiah copied around the year 200 B.C. This may have been the kind of scroll Jesus read from in the synagogue at Nazareth (see Lk 4:16–22).

Inspired. Christians believe the entire Bible, both Old and New Testaments, is inspired. This means that God used human creativity and insight to convey the religious truth God wanted communicated to us. We say that the Bible is "the word of God in the words of human beings."

Vatican II's *Dogmatic Constitution on Divine Revelation* teaches that God "made use of their [the biblical authors]

Our word *paper* comes from the word *papyrus*. The inner pith of the papyrus plant from which paper was made was called *biblos*, the root word for our word *Bible*.

powers and abilities" but they were "true authors" who "consigned to writing everything and only those things which He wanted" (No. 11).

███████████████ ■ ███████████████

Literary Forms

The Old Testament is a library of books that contain many literary forms. If you want to know what a particular biblical passage means, you should begin by identifying its literary form. For example, a newspaper editorial is a different kind of writing than a personal letter to a friend. You would interpret them differently.

We should judge, interpret, and read a literary form according to its purpose. Only then will we begin to understand what the biblical text means. For example, although the Old Testament is the written record of God's revelation to the Jews, not everything in the Bible is "history."

Below you will find some of the literary forms contained in the Old Testament. A short definition is provided for each. Please read the examples given. In the space provided, briefly explain how the example fits the definition of the form.

1. *allegory* (example: Proverbs 9:1–6): an extended comparison in which the details of a story stand for deeper realities such as abstract ideas, moral qualities, or spiritual realities

2. *biography* (example: Jeremiah 26): a written account of a person's life

3. *creed* (example: Deuteronomy 26:5–10): a formal statement of religious belief

4. *etiology* (example: Genesis 32:23–33): a story that gives the cause of something

Here are four more forms found in the Old Testament. Using a good dictionary, copy the meaning of the terms in your journal. Then, read the following passages and match them with the correct form.

Forms	Passages
riddle	Ruth 4:1–12
contract	2 Samuel 12:1–4
legend	Judges 14:12–18
parable	1 Samuel 17:1–54

5. *fable* (example: Judges 9:7–15): a brief story with a moral; often uses animals that act and speak like human beings

6. *history* (example: 1 Kings 1—2): a chronological narrative or record of events, as in the life or development of a people, country, or institution

7. *law* (example: Exodus 20:1–17): a rule of conduct or standard of behavior established by proper authority, society, or custom

8. *prophecy* (example: Amos 1—2): an inspired utterance made by a prophet which expresses God's will

Old Testament Canon

The "canon" refers to the list of biblical books that the church officially recognizes as inspired. The word *canon* comes from the Hebrew word *kaneh* which was a tall reed used to measure something, somewhat like our yardstick. The word came to mean a standard, measure, or rule. The canon of sacred scripture, therefore, is the standard list of books recognized as genuine and inspired.

Both Protestants and Catholics agree on the official list of twenty-seven books contained in the New Testament. However, we disagree on the official number of books in the Old Testament. Protestants accept only thirty-nine, while Catholics include forty-six. The discrepancy results from different ancient versions of the Jewish scriptures accepted by each group.

Catholics and the Septuagint. A Greek translation of the Jewish scriptures called the *Septuagint* was the most common and popular version of sacred scripture in New Testament times, used widely throughout the Roman Empire by both Jews and Christians.

This translation took place in Alexandria, Egypt, beginning in the third century B.C. Legend has it that seventy-two rabbis (six from each of the twelve tribes of Israel) worked independently and came up with the same translation, which was taken as a sure sign that the work was divinely inspired. The early church, important church fathers, and finally the Council of Trent (1547) accepted this translation as the standard for the Catholic Old Testament.

Protestants and the Jewish Canon.   At the time of the Protestant Reformation, the reformers adopted a canon created by Jewish rabbis around A.D. 90. In that year, Jewish scholars who had survived the Roman destruction of the Temple in A.D. 70 assembled at Jamnia, a city in northern Palestine, to consolidate their sacred books. At this meeting, they accepted only the thirty-nine books written in Hebrew. They dropped seven books that appeared in the Septuagint, which had been written in Greek sometime in the two hundred years before Christ.

The seven disputed books are *1* and *2 Maccabees, Judith, Tobit, Baruch, Sirach,* and *Wisdom.* Most Protestant Bibles today print them in a separate section at the back of the Bible and refer to them as *apocrypha,* that is, "hidden" or withdrawn from common use. Catholics refer to these books as *deuterocanonical* ("second canon") to indicate that Jews do not accept them into their official canon.

In the following chart, you will find the four major divisions of Old Testament writings, their abbreviations, and a short explanatory note about each category. Deuterocanonical works are in *italics.*

PENTATEUCH {5}

Genesis (**Gn**)
Exodus (**Ex**)
Leviticus (**Lv**)
Numbers (**Nm**)
Deuteronomy (**Dt**)

These sacred books, also known as the Torah, contain the Jewish Law and important instruction on belief and practice. They include many memorable stories of our faith: creation, Adam and Eve, Noah, Abraham and Sarah. They recount the stories of slavery in Egypt, Yahweh's covenant with the Chosen People, the Exodus, and Moses. They give us the Ten Commandments, a code of righteous living followed by Jews, Christians, and Moslems alike.

HISTORICAL BOOKS {18}

Joshua (**Jos**)
Judges (**Jgs**)
1 & 2 Samuel (**1 Sm; 2 Sm**)
1 & 2 Kings (**1 Kgs; 2 Kgs**)

1 & 2 Chronicles (**1 Chr; 2 Chr**)
Ezra (**Ezr**)
Nehemiah (**Neh**)

Ruth (**Ru**)
Esther (**Est**)
Lamentations (**Lam**)
Judith (**Jdt**)
Tobit (**Tb**)
Baruch (**Bar**)
1 & 2 Maccabees (**1 Mc; 2 Mc**)

WISDOM BOOKS {7}

Job (**Jb**)
Psalms [**Ps(s)**]
Proverbs (**Prv**)
Ecclesiastes (**Eccl**)
Song of Songs [**Song(Sg)**]
Sirach (also called
    Ecclesiasticus) (**Sir**)
Wisdom (**Wis**)

PROPHETIC BOOKS {16}

Isaiah (**Is**)
Jeremiah (**Jer**)
Ezekiel (**Ez**)

Hosea (**Hos**)
Joel (**Jl**)
Amos (**Am**)
Obadiah (**Ob**)
Jonah (**Jon**)
Micah (**Mi**)
Nahum (**Na**)
Habbakuk (**Hb**)
Zephaniah (**Zep**)
Haggai (**Hg**)
Zechariah (**Zec**)
Malachi (**Mal**)

Daniel (**Dn**)

The historical books narrate how the Chosen People lived out the covenant in the Promised Land. The first six books have the same style as the book of Deuteronomy and describe how the Promised Land was conquered and settled. They also describe the desire for monarchy, kings such as Saul and David, and the declining monarchy up to the time of the Babylonian Captivity in 586 B.C.

The next four books are written from the vantage point of a priestly writer. They relate the history of Israel from David through the Babylonian Captivity and the return under Ezra and Nehemiah.

The period after the Exile also produced some short moralistic tales to uplift and inspire the Jews. 1 and 2 Maccabees record the successful revolt of the Jews against the Greek government in Syria (168–164 B.C.).

These works contain some of the most beautiful and practical religious literature in the world. Job wrestles with the ever-current problem of suffering and good versus evil. The Psalms contain many exquisite hymns and prayers for both public and private use. The Song of Songs is an allegorical love song that treats God's love for his people. The other books offer wisdom that is often timeless in its meaning and application.

Major Prophets: The major prophets include the first three listed here. They are referred to as "major" because of the length of their books.

Minor Prophets: All the others listed. The Jewish canon calls them "The Twelve."

The prophets were powerful figures who spoke for Yahweh, often warning the people to remain faithful to the covenant or face dire consequences. Their words remain as forceful reminders of a just and faithful God who loves justice and requires believers to live faithfully and compassionately.

Daniel is in a class by itself. It is an *apocalyptic* writing containing highly symbolic language.

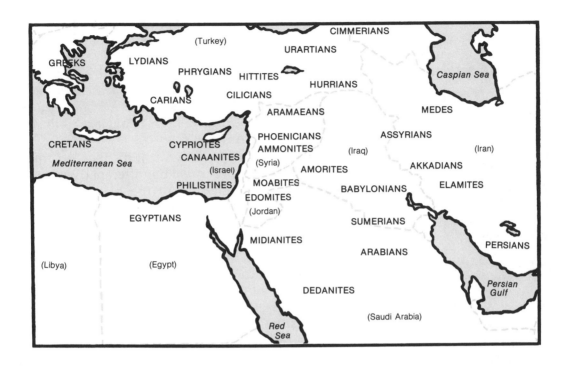

A Land and a People

Ancient Israel is the heartland of three major religions — Judaism, Christianity, and Islam. It has had many names. It was called *Canaan* when the Canaanites, a polytheistic people, were its predominant inhabitants.

Israel became its name after the twelve tribes descended from Jacob ("Israel") settled there following the Exodus. After the kingdom was divided, *Israel* referred to the northern kingdom (922 B.C until the Assyrian conquest in 721 B.C.). The southern kingdom, with its capital in Jerusalem, was known as *Judah* after the largest Hebrew tribe (Judah), which settled there. This kingdom lasted from 922 B.C. until the Babylonians conquered it in 587 B.C.

The Greeks named the country *Palestine* after Alexander the Great conquered it in 333 B.C. This designation came from the Philistines, a sea-faring people who settled along the coast. The Jews were insulted by this name for their land. *Judea*, home of the Judeans, or Jews, was the southern province, directly ruled by the Romans during the time of Jesus. Palestine was the official title until 1948 when the state of

The Jordan River is a vital source of water in the Holy Land (see also opposite page).

Israel came into being. Christians have historically referred to this area as the Holy Land because of the many places associated with Jesus.

Geographically, this area is a relatively narrow strip of land. It is roughly 150 miles long and 70 miles wide. Located at the eastern end of the Mediterranean Sea, it was an important land bridge between the three centers of ancient civilization: Egypt, Babylon, and Assyria.

To the southwest lay Egypt, a civilization that became prominent around 3000 B.C. and ruled by different dynasties of pharaohs (kings). Egypt figured in the history of the Chosen People, especially at the time of the Exodus (around 1290–1250 B.C.) when Moses led them to freedom. To the northwest, on the plains of Asia Minor, the Hittites developed an impressive civilization, though they were in major decline after 1200 B.C. To the northeast was the famous *Fertile Crescent* which embraced Mesopotamia. It gave birth to a succession of civilizations: the Sumerians (who invented writing around 3200 B.C.), the Akkadians, the Babylonians, and the Assyrians. All of these civilizations existed in the area of present-day Iraq; the Assyrians and Babylonians both figure prominently in Old Testament history. So do the Persians, a civilization that arose in what is now Iran.

Major Powers in the Ancient Near East		
Egypt (c. 1500–1200 B.C.)	Assyria (c. 1100–600 B.C.)	Babylonia (625–539 B.C.)
Persia (530–331 B.C.)	Greeks, Egyptian-Ptolemies, & Syrian- Seleucids (331–167 B.C.)	Rome (63 B.C.- A.D. 324)

Israel was both a buffer between these various powers and an important crossroads for commerce. When new powers came into this area — notably the Greeks in the fourth century B.C. and the Romans in the first century B.C. — they also recognized the strategic value of this small, but important, country.

The geographical features of their land prevented the Jews from becoming a major power in ancient times. The mountains isolated the people from one region to another, and the land itself could only support a modest population. Except for a few decades of glory during the reigns of David and Solomon, other nations invaded and overpowered Israel as a vital link in their own expanding empires.

Overview of the Old Testament Story

Before beginning our reading of the Old Testament, it would be a good idea to get an overview of the story of the Chosen People. Here are the main divisions:

1. *Ancestors of the Faith.* Genesis introduces the stories of the mothers and fathers of the Jewish faith — Abraham and Sarah, Isaac and Rebekah, Jacob and Rachel. The story opens around 1850 B.C. when God invites a wandering herdsman, Abram, to leave his country for a promised land of great prosperity. In return for God's blessing, Abraham and his descendants were to witness to the one true God. Thus begins the story of God's involvement with a special people, a story that testifies to God's loving fidelity and prepares the way for the Messiah.

2. *Exodus.* Jacob and his family settled in Egypt to escape famine in Canaan. But sometime between 1700–1250 B.C., the Egyptians enslaved the Hebrews. God, ever faithful to his promises, sent Moses to lead the people out of Egypt sometime between 1290–1250 B.C. The book of Exodus tells this story of deliverance and records the covenant between God and the people, represented by the Ten Commandments given on Mount Sinai. The Jews were to keep this Law as their part of the *covenant*; God promised to remain with the people and lead them into the Promised Land.

3. *Into Canaan.* Moses died before the Israelites crossed the Jordan River. Joshua led the people into the Promised Land and thus began a period of conquest (1250–1000 B.C.) of the various Canaanite tribes that inhabited the area. The books of Judges and Joshua describe the conquests and assimilation that took place. This is also the period of the judges, tribal heroes who defended the Israelites against the neighboring peoples. The Philistines presented a special challenge to the Chosen People, who sought a king to unify the Jewish tribes.

4. *Monarchy and Division.* Samuel, a prophet and judge, anointed the first king, Saul. Under Saul's successor, King

This stone relief of the Ark of the Covenant is found on the remains of a synagogue in Capernaum.

David, Israel became a nation recognized throughout the Middle East. David established the capital at Jerusalem and brought the Ark of the Covenant there, making it the religious center of his people. David's reign, and that of his son, Solomon, was a golden age in Jewish history. Solomon was known for his wisdom, not his military prowess. He was also a great builder, most remembered for the construction of the Jerusalem Temple.

Solomon's death brought with it the division of the kingdom into Israel and Judah in 922 B.C. Heavy taxation, enforced labor, and an arrogant style of rule upset the people. Pagan worship by some of the kings and the concentration of wealth in the hands of the upper classes outraged the prophets, who spoke on God's behalf, calling rulers and people back to true worship and justice.

5. *Destruction and Exile.* Despite the warnings of the prophets, the kingdoms of the north and the south continued to ignore God's covenant. Eventually, foreign rulers, whom the prophets saw as instruments of God's judgment, conquered both kingdoms. The northern kingdom fell to the powerful Assyrians in 721 B.C. Many inhabitants were

deported and replaced by Assyrians. The Babylonians followed the Assyrians into power and eventually conquered the southern kingdom, destroying Jerusalem in 587 B.C. This year marks the beginning of the *Babylonian Captivity* when many leading Jews were carried off to Babylon. During this period of captivity (587–538 B.C.), prophets such as Second Isaiah exhorted the people to repent and worship the one true God. They also promised God's final deliverance of his Chosen People.

6. *Return and Rebuilding.* In 538 B.C., Cyrus of Persia, who had conquered the Babylonians, allowed the Jews to return to their land. Many did so, but others had resettled throughout the Mediterranean world in what is known as the *Diaspora* or *Dispersion*. The returning exiles built a second temple (515 B.C.) and rebuilt the city. Between 450–400 B.C., priest-scholars such as Ezra consolidated the sacred writings of the people. The various histories that had previously been written were formed into the collection we know as the *Torah*, the Law. Other sacred writings, including works such as Job, Proverbs, and Tobit, were edited and composed during this period.

7. *Greece and Rome.* In 333 B.C., Alexander the Great conquered the Middle East and spread Greek culture, known as Hellenism, throughout the region. Greek culture and thought dominated the Mediterranean region from around 300 B.C.-A.D. 300. A successor to Alexander, the Syrian despot Antiochus IV, tried to impose Greek customs and practices on the Jews. He desecrated the Temple and outlawed the Torah, triggering a successful Jewish rebellion — the Maccabean Revolt — in 164 B.C. by members of the priestly Hasmonean family. The Hasmoneans ruled an independent Judea until the Roman general, Pompey, conquered Palestine in 63 B.C. A puppet king of the Romans, Herod the Great, was allowed to rule as king in Palestine from 37 B.C. until his death in 4 B.C., a year often mentioned as the year of Christ's birth.

Background Helps to Reading the Old Testament

Translations. Most of the Old Testament was written in the ancient language known as *Hebrew*. This ancient Semitic language was the living language of the Israelites until the

. *dates* .

Here are the key dates of the Old Testament story. Knowing these dates and this sequence will help you keep the events and persons of the Old Testament in perspective.

1280 B.C. — Moses, Exodus
1000 B.C. — David anointed king
922 B.C. — kingdom divided
721 B.C. — fall of northern
  kingdom to the Assyrians
587–538 B.C. — Babylonian
  captivity
164 B.C. — Maccabees cleanse
  Temple
63 B.C. — Pompey captures
  Jerusalem

astonish

13:54	so that they were astonished, and sa
19:25	they were greatly astonished, saying
22:33	they were astonished at his teaching
Mrk 1:22	they were astonished at his teaching
6: 2	many who heard him were astonishe
7:37	they were astonished beyond measur
10:26	they were exceedingly astonished, a
11:18	the multitude was astonished at his
Lke 2:48	when they saw him they were astoni
4:32	they were astonished at his teaching
5: 9	For he was astonished, and all that
9:43	all were astonished at the majesty o
11:38	The Pharisee was astonished to see
Act 13:12	he was astonished at the teaching of
Gal 1: 6	I am astonished
Jdt 11:16	things that will astonish the whole
13:17	All the people were greatly astonishe
2Mc 7:12	those . . were astonished at the youn

astonishing thing 1. פלא

Dan 11:36 speak astonishing things against the

astonishment 1. ἔκστασις

Mrk 16: 8 trembling and astonishment had com

astonishment *See also* object.

end of the Babylonian Exile. *Aramaic,* the common language spoken in Babylon and the whole Middle East, then became the language of the Jewish people. Jesus spoke Aramaic. Hebrew remained only as the sacred and literary language, although even Jews throughout the Mediterranean world from 200 B.C. used the Septuagint, a Greek translation of their scriptures.

Today, most people read the Bible in translation. In the Christian era, the common language of the Roman Empire changed from Greek to Latin. St. Jerome's Latin translation of the Old and New Testaments around the year A.D. 390, known as the *Vulgate* (meaning "common"), became the church's official translation of the Bible from original languages.

The Bible you read is, of course, an English translation. There are many English translations of the Bible available today. The first step to reading the Old Testament is to having your own copy, one you can mark up. It is helpful if this is a study Bible with good introductions and notes.

Some Tools for Studying the Old Testament. A *concordance* lists all the occurrences of a word in the Bible. Suppose you were interested in where God is called a shepherd. You could look up the word *shepherd* and find all the places it occurs. Some Bibles include a short concordance of key words in an appendix. You can also find relatively inexpensive computer programs that will do searches for every word in the Bible. Be sure to use a concordance that matches the translation of the Bible you are reading.

A good *biblical atlas* will provide some excellent maps to help you navigate around the ancient biblical world. Also, be sure to check the maps provided with many Bibles.

Most libraries contain several solid *bible dictionaries.* These reference works treat many themes, names, places, and other topics found in the Bible.

There are many excellent *commentaries* on all the books of the Bible. These commentaries can be quite scholarly, for example, the *Anchor Bible* series, or they can be designed for the beginning Bible student. An excellent multi-volume series is the *Collegeville Bible Commentary.* An outstanding one-volume commentary on the entire Bible is *The New Jerome Biblical Commentary.*

▪ *focus questions* ▪

1. Discuss four reasons for reading the Old Testament.
2. List and discuss the meaning of three key Old Testament themes that tell us how we should live.
3. What is the literal meaning of *Bible*? *testament*?
4. Explain why we should think of the Old Testament as a "library" of books.
5. What is the meaning of *biblical inspiration*?
6. List and define four literary forms used in the Old Testament. Give an example of each.
7. What is the meaning of the term *canon* of scripture? Why do Protestant and Catholic Bibles differ on the number of canonical Old Testament books?
8. Define and discuss the relationship of these two terms: *apocrypha* and *deuterocanonical*.
9. How many books are in the Catholic Old Testament? New Testament? List from memory these Old Testament books:
   a. the five books of the Pentateuch
   b. any eight historical books
   c. any three wisdom books
   d. the "major" prophets
10. What were three different names for the Promised Land during biblical times?
11. Why was Israel historically such a valuable territory?
12. Briefly identify the following persons and events that figured prominently in the history of the Chosen People: Abraham, Moses, Exodus, Joshua, Judges, David, Solomon, Divided Kingdom, Prophets, Assyrians, Babylonian Captivity, Dispersion, Torah, Hellenism, Maccabees, Pompey.
13. What happened on these dates: 1280 B.C., 1000 B.C., 922 B.C., 721 B.C., 587–538 B.C., 164 B.C., 63 B.C.
14. Identify these two translations of the Bible: *Septuagint*, *Vulgate*.
15. What reference work could help you find:
   a. a definition of the word *covenant*

b. the meaning of Psalm 23

c. the location of the word *wisdom* in the Old Testament

d. the length of the Jordan River

■ *exercises* ■

1. Consult a good Catholic biblical commentary, for example, *The New Jerome Biblical Commentary*. List five points it makes about Psalm 23.

2. Consult a biblical atlas and locate these cities: Alexandria, Nineveh, Babylon, Jericho.

3. Consult a biblical dictionary and prepare a short report on one of the following topics:

   a. key events in the life of Abraham

   b. the Dead Sea

   c. some of the meanings of the words *prophet* and *prophecy*

   d. the origination and meaning of the word *Jew*

   e. some interesting facts about *women* in Old Testament times

   f. some other topic suggested by your reading of this chapter of the text

4. Consult a concordance and find one reference in the Pentateuch for the word *faith*.

■ *vocabulary* ■

Copy the meaning of these words into the vocabulary section of your journal:

allegory   compilation
creed   etiology

■

Prayer Reflection

The God of the Hebrew scriptures, our God, is a God of promise. Staying close to God guarantees life; drifting away leads to disaster. The Bible teaches us to *choose life*. Read and reflect on these words of scripture:

"Look, today I am offering you life and prosperity....
If you obey the commandments of Yahweh your God, which I am laying down for you today, if you love Yahweh your God and follow his ways, if you keep his commandments, his laws and his customs, you will live and grow numerous, and Yahweh your God will bless you.... Choose life, then, so that you and your descendants may live, in the love of Yahweh your God,

obeying his voice, holding fast to him..." (Dt 30:15–16, 19–20).

▪ *reflection* ▪

How are you making a choice for God and life right now in your life?

▪ *resolution* ▪

Choose one of the commandments (see Dt 5:1–21), for example, "Honor your father and your mother." For the next ten days or so, review how well you live this commandment each day. If you fall short, ask for God's forgiveness and resolve once again to choose life!

chapter 2

In the Beginning...
The Pentateuch and Prehistory

God created man in the image of himself,
in the image of God he created him,
male and female he created them.

God blessed them, saying to them, "Be fruitful,
multiply, fill the earth and subdue it."

— Genesis 1:27–28

Rumor has it that a band of prominent scientists set out to research the answer to the question, "Where did the earth come from?" They represented many different academic areas: physics, geology, astronomy, chemistry, paleontology, biology, and the like.

After years of intensive study, the researchers compiled immense amounts of data from their respective disciplines and fed their findings into the world's largest and most sophisticated computer. When they finished their programming, they finally struck the "answer" button on the computer. With great anticipation they awaited the results.

Suddenly lights flashed! Bells rang! Buzzers sounded! The message that appeared said: "See Genesis 1:1."

"In the beginning God created heaven and earth" (Gn 1:1). The Bible opens with this majestic statement about the origins of the world — God is the creator of all. The first Hebrew word in the Bible means "in the beginning." The Greek Septuagint translation names this book Genesis, a word meaning "origin," because it discusses origins: of the world, of humanity, and especially of the Israelites, God's Chosen People.

The book of Genesis is part of the five-book foundation of the Jewish religion, the *Pentateuch* (Greek for "five scrolls"). The Pentateuch serves as a kind of constitution for God's people. It contains the story of how God formed his people. It also includes the various laws that the Israelites were to live in response to God's gracious blessings. Thus, the Pentateuch also bears the name *Torah* or *Law*.

The five books of the Pentateuch are:

1. *Genesis* — stories of the patriarchs of the Israelite faith: Abraham, Isaac, Jacob, and Joseph.

29

2. *Exodus* — the heart of the Torah; it highlights the story of Moses who delivered his people from slavery in Egypt and tells of God revealing his will to the Israelites in the Sinai desert and binding himself to them in a covenant.

3. *Leviticus* — the commands by which the Chosen People were to live out their part of the covenant; most of them deal with feasts, ritual sacrifice, and holiness regulations.

4. *Numbers* — laws that helped form the Israelites during their forty years in the desert before they entered the Promised Land.

5. *Deuteronomy* (Greek for "second law") — written in the form of speeches delivered by Moses, it instructs its readers on the meaning of the exodus experience. It also reminds them of the need to keep the covenant law as a sure sign of living as God's special people.

You will be reading and studying some key passages of the Pentateuch in this and the next two chapters. Our special emphasis will be on the books of Genesis and Exodus.

Who We Are

Genesis 1—11 contains many delightful stories. Scholars identify certain elements of *myth* in these stories. A myth expresses a spiritual truth or a basic belief of a particular culture by means of a narrative. These folktales use common themes and symbols such as creation near water, battles between heavenly powers, creation of humans from the earth, and the like.

The Israelites borrowed some traditional elements, symbols, and stories from the myths of their neighbors, many of whom believed in a great many gods controlling life on earth, but they radically changed them to convey their belief in the one true God — Yahweh — who was working in their history in a radical way.

Below are four key theological truths found in the biblical stories about the origins of creation, of humans, and of sin. Study these themes and reflect on their meaning in your own life.

1. Everything God makes is good, very good (Gn 1:31). This is especially true of human beings. It is true about you.

a. Are you happy with the way God made you?

   Yes   No   I'm not sure

b. What is the best thing about you?

c. If Jesus were to tell someone about you, what might he say?

2. It is not right for us to be alone. We need companions and friends (Gn 2:18).

   a. Check off three qualities you are looking for in a friend/companion:

   ____ smart   ____ rich
   ____ good-looking   ____ humble
   ____ generous   ____ compassionate
   ____ Christ-like   ____ athletic
   ____ sense of humor   ____ open
   ____ good listener   ____ forgiving
   ____ sensitive   ____ loyal
                              ____ helpful

   b. What outstanding quality do your friends find in you?

3. Take good care of the earth and the creatures in it. They are ours to use, not abuse (Gn 1:28–30). Rate yourself on these items according to this scale: **C** — I'm considerate; **N** — I need improvement; **I** — I'm inconsiderate.

   ____ a. I'm careful not to litter.

   ____ b. I conserve energy wherever possible (turn off lights, combine errands when driving, etc.).

   ____ c. I respect animals and treat them with compassion.

   ____ d. I'm careful about my own health by avoiding harmful substances.

   ____ e. I enjoy the splendor of God's creation.

4. Sin brings shame. It disrupts one's relationship with God and others. It causes inner conflict (Gn 3:1–24). When you

do something wrong, which of the following are you likely to do?

_____ a. Blame someone else.

_____ b. Lie and deny that I did it.

_____ c. Hide or cover it up.

_____ d. Admit I was wrong and ask for forgiveness.

▪ *discuss* ▪

1. What evidence can you offer for the biblical truth that what God has made is "very good"? List ten things. Emphasize what is good in human beings.

2. Construct another list that shows that something is wrong with the human condition.

▪ *journal* ▪

1. Discuss something you did that made you ashamed. Describe how it separated you from God or other people. Discuss your own feelings.

2. Describe how you did or could repair the damage you caused by this "shameful" deed.

Who Wrote the Pentateuch?

Remember... Pentateuch = Torah = Law = first five books (Gn–Dt)

The question of who wrote the first five books of the Bible has fascinated scholars for the past two centuries. Traditional belief credited Moses with writing Genesis, Exodus, Leviticus, Numbers, and Deuteronomy. Ancient rabbis and early Christians believed this. Even the New Testament assumes that Moses authored the Law. For example, Jesus explicitly calls the Pentateuch "the book of Moses" (Mk 12:26).

Today, however, we recognize that the Pentateuch took its final form only after centuries of telling, retelling, adapting, and reinterpreting the many stories of Yahweh's dealings with the Chosen People. Moses is certainly the central figure of the Pentateuch. The Israelites would naturally look to him as the source of the laws and traditions recorded in the Torah. But Moses certainly could not have written everything in these first books. For example, Deuteronomy 34:5–12 chronicles Moses' death!

The Writing of the Pentateuch

Step 1: The personality of Moses the law-giver and the events of the Exodus.

Step 2: Laws, speeches, stories, reflections, liturgical celebrations, and the like are handed down orally. Some of them are committed to writing as well.

Step 3: Authors/editors collect their sources into a continuous narrative.

Step 4: Sometime during Ezra's lifetime (c. 425 B.C.), the various traditions were brought together into the five-volume document we know as the Pentateuch.

Scholarly analysis has come up with many different theories to explain the authorship of the Pentateuch. The most popular theory suggests there were at least four major *sources* that went into the composition of the Pentateuch. The final edition of this composite work was probably completed during the life of the priest Ezra who lived between 460–400 B.C. Ezra was a leader in making the Torah a binding force in the life of all his people.

Later authors and editors did not try to reconcile all the differences in the stories and traditions that were handed down to them. They simply included their stories right after the previous author's. Or sometimes they simply added details without paying too much attention to how the final product sounded or even if it differed from a previous version.

These four traditions or sources of the Pentateuch appear in the chart below. Study it carefully.

Source/tradition: Yahwist (J); typically uses the name *Yahweh* (in German, *Jahweh*) for God.

Style: Uses the personal name *Yahweh* for God; vivid, earthy style; *anthropomorphic* view of God: "Yahweh walks and talks with us"; refers to *Mount Sinai* as the place of the Mosaic covenant; refers to natives of Israel as "Canaanites."

Where/when?   Origin in southern Israel (Judah) around 950 B.C. during the early monarchy when national pride was high.

Examples: Second creation account (Gn 2:4b–25)
Egyptian plagues (Ex 7:14—10:29)

Key themes: The divine promises made to the patriarchs:

- the blessing of Israel as a people
- the promise of their own land

Comment: The J tradition provides the basic outline of the Pentateuch: human origins, patriarchs, slavery in Egypt, the Exodus, the desert wandering, Mount Sinai covenant, and on to the Promised Land.

Source/tradition: Elohist (E); uses the term *Elohim* for God.

Style: God is *Elohim*; more abstract, less picturesque view of God; refers to *Mount Horeb* as the place of the Mosaic covenant; refers to natives as "Amorites."

Where/when?   Origin in Ephraim in the northern kingdom around 850 B.C.

Example: Abraham/Sarah (Gn 20:1–18)

Key themes: Marked by the message of Elijah and Elisha; great emphasis put on prophecy; covenant is central; God's relationship to Israel is best understood in terms of the covenant promises.

Comment: E retold J's stories from a northern point of view. The south emphasized the role of the monarchy while the north (E) was more concerned with the covenant. Abraham is a central figure in E's narrative.

Many scholars believe that around 750 B.C. an editor combined J and E into one narrative. He did not bother to drop repetitions or contradictions.

Source/tradition: Deuteronomist (D); comes from the Greek word meaning "second law."

Style: God is Yahweh; emphasis on morals and the Law; central role of several long speeches by Moses; meant to be spoken aloud to remind people of the demands of the covenant.

Where/when?   Probably composed around 650 B.C. by a priest in the northern kingdom at the shrine at Shechem. May have been finished in Jerusalem.

Example: The speeches of Moses (Dt 1:1—30:20)

Key themes: Interprets Israel's history in cylce of reward for fidelity and punishment for sin; Israel should respond to the covenant and the Law in worship; "Listen, Israel" is a constant refrain: the covenant is *now*.

Source/tradition: Priestly (P); emphasizes priestly concerns.

Style: God is Elohim; formal style; interested in census lists and genealogies; concern for numbers, dates, ways of worship, temple ceremonies, clean and unclean animals.

Where/when? Came into being during the Babylonian Exile (587–538 B.C.) to strengthen the faith and hope of the people; perhaps completed around 400 B.C.

Examples: First creation account (Gn 1:1—2:4a)
Priestly laws (Lv 1:1—27:34)

Key themes: Tremendous emphasis on worship; sees life and God's action in the history of Israel as a liturgy.

Comment: Because it was the last tradition written, P gave a coherent framework to the Pentateuch. Priestly editors under Ezra gave the first five books of the Bible their final form.

▪ *detective work* ▪

Read Gn 3:1–24. Based on the characteristics listed above, answer these two questions.

a. Which tradition (J, E, D, P) probably produced this story?

b. Give two pieces of evidence for your conclusion.

Scholarly Study of the Pentateuch

So much of the Bible deals with a time, people, and culture that are foreign to us. Thanks to the efforts of countless scholars, the world of the Bible has been opened up to all of God's people. The work of these learned men and women enables us to interpret the Bible correctly.

The basic aim of biblical interpretation is to bring together the world of the reader and the world of the biblical text in such a way that the meaning of the text makes sense to the reader. It has two essential tasks: 1) *gathering information* about the text; 2) *explaining* the meaning of the text.

Historical-Critical Method.   The Catholic faith community endorses the historical-critical method of biblical interpretation. Vatican II had this to say about interpreting scripture:

> Since God speaks in sacred Scripture...in human fashion, the interpreter of sacred Scripture, in order to see clearly what God wanted to communicate to us, should carefully investigate what meaning the sacred writer really intended, and what God wanted to manifest by means of their words.
>
> Those who search out the intention of the sacred writers must...have regard for "literary forms." For truth is proposed and expressed in a variety of ways, depending on whether a text is history,...or whether it is that of prophecy, poetry, or some other type of speech. The interpreter must investigate the meaning the sacred writer intended to express and actually expressed in particular circumstances as he used contemporary literary forms in accordance with the situation of his own time and culture (*Dogmatic Constitution on Divine Revelation*, No. 12).

The historical-critical method tries to understand biblical texts in their original setting, discovering the intention of the original author. For example, the historical-critical method will try to identify what the story of the snake talking to Adam and Eve meant to the original audience. It will also try to figure out if the teller of the story really meant us to take it literally. In addition, it will study similar stories in the ancient world and try to identify the literary form.

The following methods are used in reading and interpreting a biblical text:

- *Textual criticism* tries to reconstruct the original wording of the biblical text. It also traces the transmission of the text down through the centuries.

- *Literary criticism* analyzes the language and meaning of the text as well as examining differences in the sources.

- *Form criticism* breaks down a text into its smaller components to discover the literary forms that were used. It also explores the historical setting of these units before they appeared in the larger work.

- *Transmission history* analyzes the development of the oral traditions that were handed down. It usually studies how a story was first presented orally, then in writing, and later combined with other documents or oral traditions.

- *Redaction criticism* investigates how an editor (redactor) used written sources and what the editing tells us about the editor's theological interests.

- *Archaeology* unearths artifacts, written materials, and other evidences of the civilizations of ancient Israel and its neighbors to help us understand the world of the Bible.

Fundamentalism. You may have seen the words *fundamentalism* or *fundamentalist* in connection with some Christian groups. What do these terms refer to?

In general, a biblical fundamentalist interprets scripture in an absolutely *literal* way. A fundamentalist would say, for example, that according to the creation account in Genesis, the earth was created in seven twenty-four hour days, the equivalent of one of our weeks. This literal approach doesn't consider changes in language over the centuries and the cultural differences between our age and that of biblical times.

Reading the Bible With Understanding

Most of us must rely on the help of others in the church to answer the first question of biblical interpretation: *"What did the text mean to its original writer and audience?"*

But we can do our part to fulfill the second part of biblical interpretation: *"What does the text mean for us?"* To do this we must learn to read the Bible intelligently.

Here is a five-step "Bible-reading" plan. Use it on the reading assignment that follows.

Step 1: Choose a readable study Bible.

Step 2: Read the text to get the overall picture: What is taking place? What strikes you? What confuses you? What new ideas do you get?

Step 3: Study the text. Go back and reread the text slowly. Identify the following:

- *Who* is speaking? Who are the other people in the story?

- *What* is happening? *Why*?

- *Where* and *when* is the action, speech, event taking place?

Fit this passage into the larger context. For example, what happened before? Note any questions you might have or words you don't understand.

Step 4: Rely on helps. There are many ways to deepen your knowledge.

- Look at the introductions to the particular biblical book you are reading. Fix the passage in its historical context.
- Check the explanatory notes given in your Bible for the meaning of words and confusing passages.
- Look for cross-references that can clarify the text.
- Check the notes and hints in this text or similar introductory books to guide your reading.
- Consult a biblical atlas, dictionary, or commentary for more in-depth information.

Step 5:   Put it all together. Ask yourself these questions:
   1. What did this passage mean to its original audience?
   2. What does this passage mean to me? For example, what does it tell me about God, myself, other people, life in general?

Reading Assignment

Carefully read the two creation accounts in the first two chapters of Genesis. Fill in the following chart.

Creation accounts	Genesis 1:1—2:4a <Priestly>	Genesis 2:4b–25 <Yahwist>
1. What name does the author give the Creator?		
2. From what does God make the world?	(1:2)	(2:5–7)
3. List the order of creation.	Day 1: _____ Day 4: _____ 2: _____ 5: _____ 3: _____ 6: _____	a. _____ d. _____ b. _____ e. _____ c. _____
4. Describe the creation of humans.	(1:27)	(2:7, 21–22)
5. What should humans do?	(1:26–30)	(2:15–20)
6. The Hebrew word *ruah* means spirit, breath, wind. How is it used in each story?	(1:2)	(2:7)
7. What is the relationship between *man* and *woman* in each story?	(1:27)	(2:18–25)

Creation Accounts

The two creation accounts differ significantly in their view of God, the world, and human beings. Despite the differences, the Jews preserved both versions because of the important truths each of these stories tells us about God and creation. Let us examine these stories more carefully here.

Priestly Account (1:1—2:4a). Scholars identify P as the source of this story. The style is forceful, stately, and grand. Creation is an awesome, dramatic act by a glorious and majestic God.

The priestly author drew on the Israelites' tradition of a seven-day week, in which the seventh day, the Sabbath, was a day of rest and prayer. Creation takes place on six days. Each day represents a higher level of creation, with humans at the peak of God's design. The refrain "and God saw that it was good" marks each day. Using a parallel construction, the author distinguishes between separation and decoration: what God divides on the first three days, he "decorates" on the next three.

Separation	*Decoration*
Day 1: light from darkness	*Day 4*: bodies of light—sun, moon, stars
Day 2: sky from water	*Day 5*: birds and fish
Day 3: land from water	*Day 6*: life on land—animals and humans

The first creation account does not try to give a scientific explanation of the universe. Rather, the ancient author, under God's inspiration, drew on the knowledge of the people of his day to construct a story that reveals the following important *religious* truths:

1. *There is only one God.* Although the priestly author knew and borrowed some elements from the Babylonian creation myth known as *Enuma Elish*, he did not accept its theology of many gods, all springing from the gods of fresh and salt water, Apsu and Tiamet. The biblical author emphatically insists there is only one God and that this God created everything in existence.

2. *God planned creation.* Creation is not the result of chaotic forces or warring gods. Our God created the world in an orderly way to share life and goodness with us.

3. *Everything God made is good, very good.* The Babylonian creation story told how humans emerged from the rotting corpse of a god. Ancient peoples believed that much of material reality was evil and constantly at war with the spiritual elements in the universe. This is *not* the view of

■ *journal* ■

1. Which story is more appealing to you? Why?

2. Which story conveys more the *mystery* of God's creative act? Explain.

Jews and Christians, who see in Genesis a positive view of created reality. The biblical writer tells us that God was pleased with everything, especially with human beings made in God's own image and likeness and entrusted with responsible development of the rest of creation.

4. *The Sabbath is a special day of rest and worship.* The priestly writer tells us that God rested on the seventh day. Obviously God does not need to rest. But we, God's creatures, need to take time to be renewed by stopping our ordinary activities one day out of the week. Moreover, we need to recognize a kind and loving God as the source of our existence and worship him in prayer and thanksgiving.

These four truths forcefully state the Jewish belief about the one, powerful, good, and loving God who shares his life with his creatures.

Yahwist Account (Gn 2:4b–25). The second creation account is much lighter in tone than the first. It is down-to-earth and paints a delightful picture of a God with human qualities (*anthropomorphic*). Scholars attribute it to the Yahwist author (J) who wrote in the tenth century B.C.

This account images Yahweh as a potter who molds Adam's body like a delicate sculpture. Into this form Yahweh breathes his spirit, the breath of life. This intimate picture reveals the loving relationship between Yahweh and the first human being. Yahweh created humans before any other creatures, sharing his own life with them. This image of human and divine closeness is a radical contrast to the belief of most ancient peoples who saw God as a distant being to be feared.

The J author pictures a compassionate God who cares for Adam by making him a garden and sending him animals for companionship. God puts Adam in charge of creation by permitting him to name the animals. (In the ancient world, the power to name gave one control over what was named.) But animals do not fulfill the basic human need for companionship.

Thus J gives a further story, the creation of Eve from Adam's rib. Many see in this story a rich image of women's dignity and equality with men. This second story gives us an *etiology* of marriage, an explanation of why men and women leave their parents to form their own family. The story reveals that Yahweh wants the couple to "become one," to

enter into a close relationship that mirrors God's own relationship with them. Man and woman are equal and complementary, intended to be true companions.

The Yahwist author tells us that the man and woman felt no shame, even though they were naked. Their natural condition of intimacy with God and each other was one of total openness. Only when sin entered the picture do human beings feel ashamed and want to hide.

After examining these two creation accounts, we can better understand why the final editor of the Pentateuch was inspired to include two very different creation accounts. Together they tell us something very important about our God: *Yahweh, the awe-inspiring creator of heaven and earth (story 1), is intimately concerned with the man and woman he made the jewels of his creation (story 2).*

The Story of Sin

The Yahwist is a masterful storyteller who tackles some of humanity's most persistent and important questions, many of which revolve around sin. Someone once described sin as humanity's declaration of independence from God. This apt image summarizes well the four stories of sin told by the Yahwist in Genesis 3—11: Adam and Eve and the Fall, Cain and Abel, Noah and the Flood, and the Tower of Babel. In each of these stories, the Yahwist stresses God's judgment on sinners, but also his mercy. We find this theme brought to fulfillment in Jesus' attitude toward sinners.

Adam and Eve and the Fall (please read Genesis 3). Two truths are evident in this famous story. First, God made us to be happy, but we're not. Women suffer the pains of childbirth; men do back-breaking work to survive; nakedness causes shame; people die. Second, the all-good Creator is not responsible for this paradox. We are, and its cause is sin.

Genesis 3 uses a memorable and symbolic story to introduce the topic of sin and its consequences. Two key symbols are the serpent and the tree of good and evil. The Israelites of Moses' day considered the serpent a symbol of evil; later Jews equated it with the devil. By having the snake pose the temptation to do evil, the Yahwist author makes the important point that sin did not originally come from within humans. Sin presents itself as an outside temptation to which humans freely consent.

In Genesis 2:16–17 the author introduced us to the tree of knowledge of good and evil and Yahweh's command not to eat its fruit on pain of death. The serpent distorts the truth and deceives Adam and Eve. He promises that if they eat of the forbidden fruit, they will be like God. The forbidden fruit symbolizes knowledge only God should have — the knowledge of good and evil. Through their own willful choice, both disobeying and defying God, Adam and Eve tried to make themselves gods. Their act does indeed give them new knowledge — shame and guilt. Their self-centered choice alienates them from each other; they sense their nakedness and are ashamed. Their disobedience also alienates them from God, so they try to hide.

Note the Yahwist author's intimate style when talking about the Lord who walks in the garden looking for the man and the woman "in the cool of the day" (3:8). When questioned about his behavior, Adam blames Eve. Eve, in turn, blames the snake. But the truth is Adam and Eve made a free and defiant choice.

The story tells us that sin also alienates us from nature. It is the cause (etiology) of sweat-producing work, painful childbirth, and death. But most important, sin keeps us from close intimacy with God, symbolized by banishment from the garden.

However, Yahweh still loves his disobedient children. God condemns the evil one and promises that one day the serpent will be destroyed by the offspring of the woman. Christians see in this hope-filled promise the person of Jesus Christ, who came to defeat the devil and his power. Another sign of God's care for his children is that he garbs them in leather garments and settles them outside the garden. Though the original harmony and intimacy has been upset, God will never abandon them.

■ *discuss* ■

1. What was the real sin of Adam and Eve? Disobedience? Pride? Something else?
2. How do you define sin? What causes it?
3. Discuss several examples of the tendency to blame one's sins on something or someone else.
4. "If it feels good, do it." Discuss how this rationalization for behavior is similar to the appeal of the snake in the story.

What's in a Name?

1. What is the meaning of the word *Eve* (3:20)?
2. What is the meaning of the word *Adam* (2:7)?

■

Self-Reflection on Sin

1. Rank these sources of temptation for you (1 — most serious).

    _____ peer pressure

    _____ something you read, saw, or heard

    _____ your own fantasies (thoughts, imagination)

    _____ your strong, uncontrolled emotions

    _____ other: _____

2. When you sin, what do you typically do? (Check one.)

    _____ make excuses

    _____ blame someone else

    _____ deny that I did any wrong at all

    _____ accept full responsibility

    _____ other: _____

■

Cain and Abel (please read Gn 4:1–16).   The story of Cain and Abel shows that human beings, when left to their own devices, degenerate into sin. The story shows how sin leads to the murder of a brother. Abel, whose offering was more pleasing to Yahweh, is portrayed as a shepherd, while Cain is a farmer. This reflects the conflict between the early Israelites, who were shepherds, and the more settled Canaanite farmers who already occupied the Promised Land.

Out of jealousy, Cain kills his brother. As punishment, Yahweh banishes him from the land and condemns him to a life of wandering. But, again, God does not abandon the sinner. The "mark of Cain" symbolizes God's concern even for the one severely punished. According to the Yahwist, the sins of humanity are terrible, punishment is swift and just, but punishment does not mean abandonment. The Lord is a God of fidelity and love. This basic theme occurs again and again in the Yahwist sections of the Pentateuch.

The Flood (please read Gn 6:5—9:29).   A careful reading of the account of the flood in Genesis will quickly reveal many repetitions and discrepancies. The explanation is simple: The story interweaves both the Yahwist (J) and the Priestly (P) versions. Compare Genesis 6:13–22 to 7:1–5 for an example of this repetition. Also note in these verses a major discrepancy in the number of animals Noah is supposed to take on board the ark. P's version (6:19–20) reports God telling Noah to take *one pair* of every species while J's instruction (7:2–3) is to take *seven pairs* of clean animals and one pair of unclean animals.

For both J and P to report the flood story suggests its importance. Even though most scholars believe the flood story is symbolic, it may have its source in a real catastrophe in the mists of history. Babylon and Syria also had flood stories similar to the Noah story. The most famous parallel is the Epic of Gilgamesh where the gods instruct the hero to build an ark and take animals on it before they destroy the world. Like Noah, Gilgamesh's hero — Utnapishtim — sends out birds, gets stuck on a mountain, eventually leaves the ark, and offers sacrifice to the gods. And for his efforts, the gods bless Utnapishtim with immortality.

The Bible's version, however, tells us why God wished to destroy the earth: human wickedness and depravity. Second, Noah does not gain immortality. Rather, God blesses Noah and instructs him and his children to repopulate the earth. Bringing to mind the creation of Adam, Noah is instructed to be fertile, multiply, be master of the animals, and subdue the earth. Again, we can see here the way biblical authors used elements from the stories and myths of other traditions to make specific theological points.

God's love for Noah is reflected in the first biblical covenant. We shall see in future chapters how the notion of covenant developed through Israel's history. Here God promised that a flood would never again destroy the earth or all its people. The sign of this covenant is the rainbow, a symbol of the Lord's presence. It is a reminder to everyone that God continues to love humanity despite its sinful nature which demands correction and punishment. Every time we see a rainbow, we should remember God's presence in creation and love for us despite our weakness. It symbolizes God's promise to bless us abundantly.

Tower of Babel (please read Gn 11:1–9).   The Tower of Babel combines two stories that illustrate humanity's defiance of

■ *journal* ■

1. Why is the dove with an olive branch a traditional symbol of peace and harmony?
2. A rainbow symbolizes God's presence in our lives. Briefly comment on three "rainbows" in your life that speak of God's care for you.
3. Read Gn 9:18–28. Who were Noah's sons? What sin did the youngest commit?

■ *discuss* ■

Why is being disrespectful of one's parents a serious offense?

God. The first is about the building of a tower, probably a Mesopotamian-type temple known as a *ziggurat*. The Babylonians constructed these elaborate temple altars to worship their god, Marduk. The second story describes humanity's attempt to build a civilization in defiance of God's command to disperse and populate the earth.

The extreme ambition reflected in this story, the people's desire to "make a name" for themselves, was a foolish act of pride. The increasing desire to create a culture apart from God resulted in alienation from God and discord among people. Again, Genesis returns to one of its major themes: Rebellion and "going it alone," isolated from God, results in punishment and separation.

In the Babel story, the Yahwist author uses a clever play on the Hebrew word *balal*, "confusion," to explain the etiology of the different languages among the world's diverse people. *Babel* (the Hebrew word for Babylon) is the place where human pride caused the Lord to confuse the speech of the world. Defying God brings about indescribable consequences such as difficulty in human communication and cooperation.

Prehistory ends with the Tower story. Sin leaves people confused and scattered around the world. But once again, God does not abandon humanity. Genesis gives us a genealogy that begins with Noah's son, Shem, and ends with the patriarch Abraham. Through Abraham, God would create the Chosen People and bless all their generations to the end of time.

▪ *focus questions* ▪

1. What is the meaning of the word *Genesis*?
2. What is the meaning of the word *Pentateuch*?
3. Briefly identify and describe the contents of the Pentateuch.
4. What is a *myth*? How does the Bible use myths?
5. Identify the following: J, E, D, P.
6. What was a major theme or concern of *each* of the *sources* of the Pentateuch?
7. What are the two basic goals of *biblical interpretation*?
8. What does the historical-critical method of biblical scholarship try to do?

9. Identify the term *fundamentalist.*

10. Which type of biblical criticism answers the following questions:

    a. How did the editor of the text use his materials?

    b. What is the original wording of the text?

    c. What sources did the author of the text use?

11. Discuss several steps you should take to read and understand a biblical passage.

12. Discuss several truths the creation stories reveal about God and the world.

13. Why did the final editor of the Pentateuch include two different creation stories?

14. According to the story of the Fall, what are several results of sin?

15. What was the nature of the first sin? How did it come about?

16. What is the ray of hope after God's punishment of Adam and Eve and Cain?

17. How do the biblical authors understand the purpose of the Flood?

18. What covenant did the Lord make with Noah and what is its sign?

19. According to the Tower of Babel story, what wrongdoing caused God to confuse the languages of people?

▪ *exercises* ▪

1. Locate in the newspaper a story about a crime, social problem, or tragedy that shows pride or defiance as the root of the problem. List three bad results of the "sinful" situation.

2. Find a magazine article on evolution and the Bible. Report on whether the author believes that the Bible and science can be reconciled. If the article holds that evolution is a false theory, list the arguments used to prove the literal truth of the Bible.

3. Using a photo of your favorite scenic area, write a short prayer-poem that praises God for his work of art.

▪ *vocabulary* ▪

Copy the meaning of these words into the vocabulary section of your journal.

anthropomorphic   paleontology
discrepancy   paradox

Prayer Reflection

The Book of Psalms holds a special place in the Bible. The 150 psalms include hymns, passionate appeals to God, and joyous cries of thanksgiving. Christians and Jews alike treasure this special collection for its depth of feeling and timeless beauty. We will draw on the psalms for many of our prayer reflections throughout this book. Read them slowly. Say them aloud. Let the words of the ancient psalmists become your own words.

Psalm 8 is a three-part hymn of praise: First, it sets a tone of praise; second, it gives reasons for praising God; finally, it concludes with a blessing.

> Yahweh our Lord,
> how majestic is your name throughout the world!
>
> Whoever keeps singing of your majesty higher than the
>   heavens,
> even through the mouths of children, or of babes in
>   arms,
> you make him a fortress, firm against your foes,
> to subdue the enemy and the rebel.
>
> I look up at your heavens, shaped by your fingers,
> at the moon and the stars you set firm —
> what are human beings that you spare a thought for
>   them,
> or the child of Adam that you care for him?
>
> Yet you have made him little less than a god,
> you have crowned him with glory and beauty,
> made him lord of the works of your hands,
> put all things under his feet,
>
> sheep and cattle, all of them,
> and even the wild beasts,
> birds in the sky, fish in the sea,
> when he makes his way across the ocean.
>
> Yahweh our Lord,
> how majestic your name throughout the world!

Think about yourself as the crowning achievement of God's creation. Note in your journal fifteen words that describe your outstanding traits, the jewels in your crown of "glory and beauty."

resolution

Every morning for the coming week, look in the mirror and thank God for what you see there. Tell the Lord that you will remember all day how special you are.

chapter 3
Creation of a People
Ancestors in the Faith

Yahweh said to Abram, "Leave your country, your kindred and your father's house for a country which I shall show you; and I shall make you a great nation, I shall bless you and make your name famous; you are to be a blessing!

> I shall bless those who bless you,
> and shall curse those who curse you,
> and all clans on earth
> will bless themselves by you."
>
> — Genesis 12:1–3

Imagine a fire in a two-story house. On the second floor is the bedroom of a six-year-old boy. His mother and father, whose bedroom is on the first floor, are barely able to escape to the safety of their front lawn. The flames prevent the father from re-entering the house to rescue his son who has made it to the bedroom window. Help is at least five minutes away. How will the child escape?

The father shouts up to his son who cannot see him, "Don't be afraid. Jump out of the window. I'll catch you."

By now the neighbors have gathered around. To their relief, the boy jumps. Gasps are heard. But his father catches him. Totally trusting and relaxed, the boy fell unharmed into his father's arms.

This is a story of faith in action. The boy heard his father's voice and believed he was there even though he could not see him. Furthermore, he trusted that his father would catch him. Finally, he obeyed his father's command to step out of the window. The little boy exhibited the three main ingredients of true faith: belief, trust, and obedience. This strong faith saved his life.

This chapter of our journey through the Hebrew scriptures focuses on a person of faith — Abraham — and his family. They exhibited the same kind of faith as the boy in our story. Abraham, his wife Sarah, their children, and their children's children trusted in a loving God who promised them a land and a people. Their fidelity to God's promise helped create God's Chosen People.

51

---- ■ ----

Faith Survey

Genesis 12—50 introduces Abraham and his family, our ancestors in faith and the first of the Chosen People. Abraham's faith enabled God to accomplish the divine will in human history.

Examine your own faith life. Circle one answer for each of the following statements. Keep in mind that there are no absolute answers.

A = agree   **NS** = not sure   **D** = disagree

1. If I have faith, then I won't doubt God.   A   NS   D
2. If I could witness a miracle, my faith would increase.   A   NS   D
3. If I am having rough times, it is probably because I don't have enough faith.   A   NS   D
4. My faith helps me live my daily life.   A   NS   D
5. I believe God answers my prayers.   A   NS   D
6. I believe Jesus has invited me to eternal life.   A   NS   D

■ *discuss* ■

1. Share your responses to several of your choices above.

2. Name a person you know who has very strong faith. Discuss some of the outstanding qualities of this person.

3. Share a time when your faith helped you.

■ *journal* ■

Look up the following New Testament passages and complete the sentences in your own words.

Heb 11:1 — Faith is . . .

Rom 10:17 — Faith comes from . . .

Jas 2:18–19 — We show our faith when . . .

In a short paragraph, list and discuss three of your own beliefs.

---- ■ ----

Historical Background

When we compare Genesis 1—11 to Genesis 12—50 we notice a definite shift in focus. The first eleven chapters of Genesis poetically describe primeval history, the world as God intended it to be and what human sinfulness made of it. Chapter 12 represents a turning point. There we find God's revelation to a special man, Abram (later renamed *Abraham*, "father of a multitude") and God's invitation to him to leave the country of his kinfolk and travel to a new land. From this historical person God established a community, the people of Israel.

Historically Accurate?   How are we to take the stories of Abraham, Isaac, Jacob, Joseph, their wives and families? How reliable are they, especially when we consider that the Israelites did not commit them to writing until the time of the monarchy, a thousand years after Abraham died? Scholars acknowledge that these stories contain many elements of folklore. Tribes took pride in their ancestors and delighted in exaggerating their deeds. Storytellers drew on their vivid imaginations to record conversations among the central characters in their tales. Legendary elements were attached to holy places, and the names of towns were related to various prominent ancestors.

It is impossible to identify precise historical truth in these stories. According to one theory, the heroes of Genesis 12—50 might have been the leading figures in various nomadic clans. According to this explanation, around the eighteenth century B.C., these clans formed an alliance. In addition, they worshiped the same God — El — and blended the customs and traditions of the various tribes.

Based on Historical Traditions.   Although these stories contain folklore and elements of uncertain historical value, most biblical scholars and archaeologists agree that they rest on real historical persons and tribes that date back to the Middle Bronze Age (2300 — 1600 B.C.). Facts recorded in the biblical stories about marriage customs, legal contracts, travel, and the lifestyle of semi-nomadic peoples all did take place during this period.

No one doubts the historical existence of Abraham who originally came from the Sumerian city of Ur. His people were probably the *Amorites* ("Westerners"), a Semitic people

■ *research* ■

The word Semite derives from Noah's son Shem, ancestor to Abraham. The Israelites and many other tribes in the ancient Near East were Semitic peoples.

What is the meaning of the word anti-Semitic?

that began to migrate westward out of Mesopotamia around 2100 B.C. Abraham himself probably lived around 1800 B.C. After migrating to Haran in modern-day Syria, Abraham made his way down to Canaan, a land the Canaanites had already inhabited for around a thousand years.

The Canaanites had settled in large, fortified city-states in the fertile Jordan River valleys. In contrast, Genesis tells us that Abraham, Isaac, and Jacob and their families lived a semi-nomadic lifestyle near the large cities, but not in them. They kept flocks of sheep and goats in semi-permanent encampments, but often uprooted their tents to lead their flocks to greener pastures as conditions dictated. The social life of these people was family and clan oriented rather than urban.

The ancient ancestors of the faith are both sinful and saintly. For example, Abraham rather cowardly sacrificed his wife's honor to save his own life. However, to save Sodom from destruction, he also bargained with God like a bazaar merchant. Despite his shortcomings, however, Abraham never doubted God's promise of descendants and a land.

The stories of these people show us again and again that divine grace works through human flaws. For example, Jacob displayed trickery and double-dealing, but God turned him into a person of integrity. And Joseph psychologically tormented his brothers to revenge their betraying him, but eventually he identified himself as their brother and saved their lives. Rebekah promotes a favorite son against the wishes of her husband. Unknown to her, her scheming ways helped God's plan unfold.

God used these very human personalities to accomplish the divine will: the creation and preservation of a special people who will reveal God to all the nations.

The surface details of the stories tell us about tribal ancestors, the etymology of place names, the triumphs and setbacks of Israel's heroic ancestors, and the like. Beneath the surface, though, they reveal a loving God, close to the Chosen People, revealing himself in dreams, in fire, and in special messengers. This personal God enters into a covenant relationship with Abraham and his descendants. This God is the only true God, radically different from the many gods of the other tribal peoples, gods who need to be placated by various superstitious rituals. The God of Abraham is a God who protects and cherishes.

Each of the literary traditions in Genesis found something of value in these stories. The Yahwist stressed the promise of blessing. The Elohist, who worried about his contemporaries abandoning God to worship false Canaanite gods, highlighted Abraham and Jacob as models of faith in the one true God. The Priestly author, who probably wrote during the Babylonian Exile, recalled God's promise to Abraham. Despite setbacks, God will rescue us and keep his word.

God's Name

Genesis is fascinated with names, their derivations and meanings. When we name something, we have a certain power over what is named. To reveal our name is to reveal something very intimate about ourselves. After Jacob wrestled with God and demanded to know God's name, God refused to tell him. God is above and beyond all creatures. God is unknowable. We do not know God's personal name; we have no power over God. The following are three ways God is referred to in scripture.

El, Elohim: The Chosen People used a common Semitic name, *El*, to refer to God. Originally, the Canaanites had a god named *El*, the father of all other gods and of all creatures. *Elohim* is a plural form of *El*.

No one knows the original meaning of *El*. The Chosen People typically spoke of God as the "God of Abraham, of Isaac, of Jacob" and the like. God was known by what he meant to those who worshipped and developed a covenant relationship with him.

El Shaddai: A popular designation of God in Genesis is *El Shaddai*, often translated as "God Almighty." This is a mistranslation. The title *Shaddai* probably came from Abraham's ancestors and may have meant "God of the mountain" or "God of the open wastes." (Check verses 17:1, 28:3, 35:11, 43:14, 48:3, and 49:25 to see how your version of the Bible translates this word.)

Yahweh: As we saw in the last chapter, the **J** author of Genesis uses the name Yahweh to refer to God from the beginning of history, though the **P** and **E** traditions tell us that this name is only revealed to Moses on Mount Horeb (Ex 3). Scholars are not sure how to pronounce the name, since out of respect for Almighty God, the Jews never pronounced it. The word appeared as **YHWH** in the sacred writings of the Jews (called the Tetragrammaton, Greek for "four letters"). Instead of reading or saying the divine name aloud, the Israelites substituted the word *Adonai* (translated *Lord*). (The combination of the vowels of Adonai, a-o-a, were added to create the hybrid word *Jehovah*, which you will sometimes find in older translations of the Bible.)

No one knows for sure what **YHWH** means. It probably comes from some form of the Hebrew word "to be," thus underscoring God's majestic and mysterious presence. The Latin Vulgate translation is "I am who am," while the Septuagint renders the sacred name, "He who is."

▪ *research project* ▪

Each religion tries to name God given its own experience. Select one of the following religions or cultures and find its name(s) for God—or choose another culture that has meaning for you. What does the name mean in the context of that culture?

Islam	Ancient Greek
Hindu	Ancient Norse
Navajo	

Write a short report summarizing your findings.

Let us turn now to some of the highlights that reveal God's promise to humanity through Abraham and his descendants.

Abraham's Story

Picture Abram gazing at a starry sky somewhere on a plain near the ancient upper Mesopotamian city of Haran. The awesome size of the universe strikes him as he reflects on his own very small place in it. But on that fateful evening under the stars, or perhaps later in a dream, God met Abram in the depths of his soul.

That first encounter between God and Abram was like the planting of a seed. God touched an individual and blessed him. Through Abram God would build a family and then a nation. And through them, God would stretch out his saving hand to all of humanity. Five words summarize Abram's remarkable story: call, faith, journey, covenant, and fulfillment.

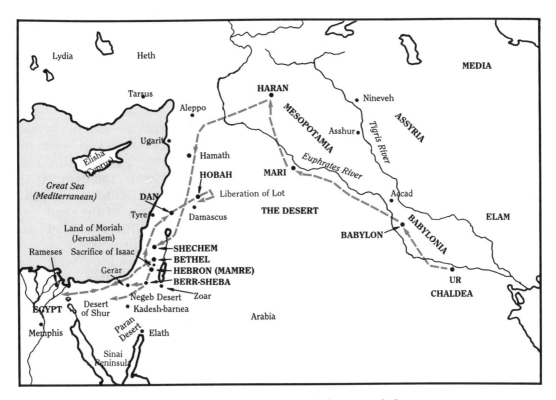

Abram's Call, Faithful Response, and Journey (please read Gn 12—13). God's special call to Abram, which we read in Gn 12:1–3, blesses him and promises him that a great nation would emerge from him and his descendants.

Abram *heard* God's call, *believed* it, and *obeyed.* Hearing, believing, and obeying God comprise the virtue of faith. Abram journeyed in faith to Shechem in the land of Canaan. God appeared to Abram again and made still another promise, "I shall give this country to your progeny" (12:7). Abram believed, but he did not settle in Shechem. Rather, he continued his journey first to Bethel, to Ai, and then into the Negeb region. Because of famine in Canaan, Abram moved his family to Egypt. While in Egypt Abram deceived the pharaoh by claiming that his beautiful but childless wife Sarai was his sister. Abram may have been invoking an ancient custom of his people to adopt a wife as a sister to give her a higher status. But he also feared that if the Egyptians knew Sarai was his wife, they would kill him in order to take her. His deception permitted the pharaoh to take Sarai into his royal harem, thus jeopardizing God's promise that Sarai would bear *Abram's* child. Abram's hesitation in seeing how

God would protect him exemplifies the inclination we all have to control our own destiny.

When the pharaoh's household is struck with severe plagues, he returns Sarai to Abram. God did not allow anything to threaten the divine promises. The Lord is faithful, always watching out for his chosen ones.

Having been banished from Egypt for his deception, Abram again was on the move. He journeyed with his nephew Lot back to Canaan. Both men had large flocks so they had to split up to keep peace between their respective families. Abram, though older and by right having prior claim, generously allowed Lot first choice of the land. Lot chose the lush and fertile lands near Sodom, a town that later became known for its perverted sexual customs.

One more time the Lord promised the land to Abram and assured him of descendants more numerous than the "dust on the ground." By walking the length and breadth of the land, Abram symbolically took legal possession of it, although it was not yet his.

Covenant (please read Gn 15—20). In Genesis 15 God's word came to Abram in a dream. Although Abram was without a child, God again promised him descendants as numerous as the stars. Our writer tells us: "Abram put his faith in Yahweh and this was reckoned to him as uprightness" (15:6).

God entered into a covenant with Abram, assuring him that the divine word would come about. To seal the covenant, Abram split in two some sacrificial animals and walked between the two halves. The "flaming torch," a sign of God's presence, also passed between the animals. This ritual, common in the ancient world, emphasized that either party would rather be killed and dismembered than break their solemn promise. It also symbolized that both God and Abram entered into a solemn contractual agreement by which God promised Abram a land, descendants, and his continuous friendship with Abram's people.

The Lord repeats this pledge in Genesis 17. He changed Abram's name to *Abraham* to signify that he would be the "father of a multitude." The Lord also changes Sarai's name to *Sarah* (meaning "princess"). For his part, Abraham and his descendants must believe in the Lord's word and be circumcised as a sign of the covenant.

Sarah's barrenness caused her to doubt God's promise. According to an ancient custom of the time, she offered her maid Hagar to Abraham so he could have a son. Abraham did have sexual relations with Hagar who conceived a son, Ishmael. Abraham finally had an heir, but by his own efforts, rather than according to the Lord's will.

Fulfillment (Gn 21—23).   Once more the Lord promises a son, but both Abraham and Sarah found this laughable because of their advanced age. But the Lord was true to his word: Sarah did indeed give birth to a son, Isaac, a name that means "laughter." The Lord always has the last laugh; the divine will shows its utter graciousness.

Abraham has revealed himself as a complex person of faith. He was obedient to God, embarking on the adventure of traveling to a new land. His resourcefulness took him to Egypt during a famine, his cunning saved his life at the pharaoh's hand, his generosity gave Lot valuable pastures.

He was also a just man, deeply committed to the protection of innocent life. We see this trait in Abraham's passionate appeal to save Lot's town of Sodom and other towns from God's wrath. Though the towns were notoriously sinful, Abraham pleaded for the innocent people there: "'Do not think of doing such a thing: to put the upright to death with the guilty, so that upright and guilty fare alike! Is the judge of the whole world not to act justly?'" (Gn 18:25).

Yahweh assured Abraham that he would spare Sodom if there were only ten innocent people in the city. But so thoroughly wicked were these towns that Yahweh permitted an earthquake to level them. Only Lot and his family were spared. Abraham's intervention moved God: "Thus it was that, when God destroyed the cities of the plain, he did not forget Abraham and he rescued Lot from the midst of the overthrow, when he overthrew the cities where Lot was living" (Gn 19:29).

Test of Faith (please read Gn 21—23).   Abraham's real character strength was his faith. When the Lord tested the quality of Abraham's faith by ordering him to offer up his beloved son Isaac in sacrifice, Abraham proved himself worthy of Yahweh's blessing (Gn 22). Though his faith was severely tested, Abraham committed himself to his God. He *trusted* and *obeyed* without protest, bargaining, or hesitation. He prepared to sacrifice his son, but at the last minute, the Lord's messenger stopped the sacrifice. Abraham had proven his faith.

The traditional site of Sarah's burial plot

There are many levels of meaning in this story. The Israelites saw in it God's condemnation of child sacrifice, a practice engaged in by some of their neighbors. Both Jews and Christians see in Abraham a person of strong faith who put aside his own doubts to follow his Lord. Isaac, too, had faith in his father and in God's will. He trusted, believed, and obeyed Abraham. Christians also believe that Isaac prefigures the perfect victim, Jesus Christ, who offered his life for all people.

Abraham's Death. "Yahweh had blessed Abraham in every way" (Gn 24:1) as his years came to an end. Abraham tenderly buried his wife Sarah and found a wife for Isaac. Chapter 23 tells us how Abraham, a resident alien in Canaan, bargained successfully to buy a burial plot for his wife. By doing so he established a small but valid land right in the Promised Land.

In chapter 24, Abraham sent a servant to his home country to find a bride for Isaac. Led by God, the servant returned with the lovely Rebekah whom Isaac married. Thus, when Abraham died at the old age of 175 years, the promises made to him were being fulfilled. He had a son by Sarah, he had claim to land in Canaan, and his son was ready to begin his own family. After Abraham's death, God continued to bless Isaac (Gn 25:11).

▪ discuss ▪

What do you find most admirable in Abraham, our father in faith?

▪ journal ▪

Read these passages about Jacob and list ten words or phrases about the Jacob you meet there.

- Gn 25:19–34 (Esau/Jacob)
- Gn 27 (Jacob's deception)
- Gn 28:10–22 (Jacob's dream)
- Gn 29—30 (Jacob, Rachel, Laban)
- Gn 32:23–33 (Jacob's wrestling match)

▪ journal ▪

1. Do one of the following:
   - Pretend you are Abraham. Describe the thoughts and feelings you had when God ordered you to sacrifice your son.
   - Pretend you are Isaac. Describe this fateful day from your point of view.
2. Write about a time when your faith was put to the test. What did you do? How did you feel at the time?

Isaac and Jacob

Genesis 24 describes the beautiful marriage between Rebekah and Isaac. Rebekah, like Sarah before her, was barren, but Yahweh heard Isaac's prayer on his wife's behalf. Rebekah conceived, but her joy soon turned to grief as the children inside her tossed and turned so much it made life miserable. Yahweh revealed to her the source of her turmoil. She bore two sons who would father two rival nations, with one nation superior over the other just as the older son would serve the younger.

Twins.   The elder twin, who was hairy and reddish, was named Esau, a name meaning "reddish." He would father the Edomites (a word meaning reddish) who lived in the region of Seir (a word meaning hairy), across the Dead Sea. They were a chief rival to the Israelites when they settled in that area.

Genesis 27:36 suggests that Jacob gets his name from his trickery toward Esau. However, his name probably derives from a word that means "May God protect."

Esau and Jacob grew up at odds with one another. Esau was a hunter, probably wild and boisterous. Jacob was a shepherd who lived in a tent and was probably more civilized. Isaac favored the older Esau, while Rebekah cherished Jacob.

Jacob, in fact, was a trickster of the first class. He tricked Esau into selling his birthright for a hearty portion of Jacob's stew. The near-blind Isaac fully intended to give a death-bed blessing to his favorite son, Esau. This blessing was so sacred that, according to ancient belief, the one giving it could not revoke it. Rebekah overheard Isaac's plan and instructed Jacob to conspire with her to trick Isaac into blessing him. She even agreed to accept any curse her husband would utter when he found out about the deception.

Although Isaac was suspicious when he heard Jacob's voice, he was sure it was Esau when he felt and smelled the outdoor odor on the hairy garments Jacob wore. He pronounced the sacred blessing. Genesis shows how the Lord worked even through this deception to fulfill the divine choice of Jacob. This blessing was sweet to the descendants of Jacob, the Israelites, who must have repeated it often around campfires:

> Ah, the smell of my son
>   is like the smell of a fertile field
>   which Yahweh has blessed.
> May God give you
>   dew from heaven,
>   and the richness of the earth,
>   abundance of grain and wine!

> Let peoples serve you
> and nations bow low before you!
> (Gn 27:27b–29a).

Both Esau and Isaac were furious when they found out the lie. Jacob had supplanted Esau twice — first his birthright, then his blessing. Esau swore murderous revenge on his brother. As a result, Rebekah thought it wise to send Jacob back to her brother Laban's country to find a wife of his own.

Jacob and Yahweh.   While traveling toward Haran where his kinfolk lived, Jacob had his first significant experience of God. Sleeping outdoors with a stone for a pillow, he dreamed of a ladder reaching from the earth to heaven. Angels were going up and down it. Yahweh appeared in the dream and identified himself as the God of Abraham and the God of Isaac. The Lord also repeated the promises of the covenant with Abraham. In addition, the Lord promised Jacob safety on his journey. So impressed was Jacob with the holiness of this sacred place that he renamed it Bethel, "gate of heaven."

However, at this point of his life, the self-assured Jacob was not yet ready to commit himself totally to Yahweh. He vowed that if God kept him safe on his journey, provided food and clothes, and helped him arrive safely in the land of his ancestors, Yahweh would be his God. He was to learn the hard way that not he but God was in control of events.

Jacob Finds a Wife.   Jacob eventually made it to Haran where he immediately fell in love with the beautiful Rachel, the daughter of his uncle Laban. Laban allowed Jacob to work for him for seven years to earn the hand of Rachel in marriage. On the wedding night, Laban substituted his heavily veiled oldest daughter, Leah, for Rachel. Jacob did not discover the ruse in his dark tent and so he spent his first night with the wrong wife.

Naturally, Jacob was furious with the deception. Laban explained that it was customary to marry the oldest daughter first. He told Jacob that he could also marry Rachel in exchange for another seven years of hard work. Jacob loved Rachel so much that he agreed to the terms.

Jacob fathered many children with his wife Leah, her servant, and with Rachel's servant, but his beloved Rachel was unable to conceive. Finally, Rachel gave birth to a son, Joseph. It was now time for Jacob to return to the land promised to him by Yahweh. Jacob enriched himself at Laban's expense through a cunning plan to build a flock of sheep. Because of the deception, he left Laban's territory hastily and in secret.

Laban eventually caught up with him and sought to reclaim some household idols Rachel had taken with her. But Yahweh appeared to Laban in a dream and warned him not to harm Jacob. Laban made a non-aggression covenant with Jacob, settling the borders between their respective lands.

Jacob Returns to Canaan.   On his way to Canaan, Jacob heard that Esau was sending four hundred men to meet him. This alarmed Jacob, who prepared his camp for an attack by his revengeful brother. However, he also resorted to prayer, reminding God of his promises of protection.

Before meeting his brother, Jacob had a strange meeting with a mysterious person who wrestled with him all night. Jacob persisted in this test of wills and refused to let go until he received a blessing from his opponent. Instead, Jacob is given a new name — *Israel* — meaning "one who contends with God." The mysterious stranger did not reveal his name, but Jacob was sure that he met God face to face. This meeting was a special blessing on Jacob, transforming him from a crafty, deceptive person into an honorable man.

Much to Jacob's relief, Esau was happy to see him. But the brothers went their separate ways, with Jacob moving to the ancient city of Shechem where he erected a memorial stone to God. At God's promptings, he next moved his family to Bethel. But first Jacob asked his family to purify themselves, ridding themselves of anything connected with paganism. When they arrived at Bethel, he erected an altar to Yahweh on the very spot where God first appeared to him. Jacob had initiated his family into the proper worship of Yahweh.

The Jacob stories conclude with Yahweh once again renewing the covenant. We see that Yahweh fulfilled his promises: Jacob found a home in Canaan, the Promised Land. And his family was large and growing in numbers.

Joseph and His Brothers

Some of the most interesting and dramatic stories in the Old Testament revolve around Jacob's twelve sons, especially his favorite son, Joseph (Gn 37, 39—50). The Yahwist was the first to put these in writing. He took various stories about Joseph, Israel's earliest days in Egypt, and certain traditions about some of the brothers and tribes and wove them into a literary masterpiece. The story has elements of adventure, intrigue, romance, and suspense.

The main outline of the story is simple. It begins with a petty family quarrel that ultimately set in motion a series of events that led to Jacob and his family moving to Egypt. The story opens with a report that Jacob loved Joseph more than any of the other brothers. One night this favored son had a dream which he interpreted for his brothers: *they* would have to serve *him*. The brothers resented the implication. They also disliked Joseph for circulating bad reports about them to their father. When Jacob had a long tunic (a sign of special esteem) made for Joseph, the brothers took offense at his obvious favoritism. First they planned to kill Joseph, but then they conspired to sell him into slavery.

Dothan's Well — traditional site of the attack on Joseph by his brothers

An Ishmaelite caravan took Joseph to Egypt where he was sold as a slave to Potiphar, the chief steward of the pharaoh. Joseph's charming manners and intelligence soon won him favor with his new master. But Joseph fell victim to Potiphar's wife for refusing her attempts at seduction. She falsely accused him before Potiphar, and he ended up in prison. There, he successfully interpreted the dreams of some fellow prisoners and established a reputation as an interpreter of dreams.

Eventually, the pharaoh heard of Joseph's gifts. When Joseph warned the pharaoh of an approaching famine, he was made chief governor of Egypt and is credited with preparing the country for the famine. He took an Egyptian wife who bore him two sons, Manasseh and Ephraim. These sons would inherit his birthright and father two important Israelite clans.

The famine Joseph predicted finally came. It brought Joseph's brothers to Egypt in search of grain to take back to their country. They did not recognize Joseph, who at first strung them along in a game of intrigue. Joseph accused them of being spies. He ordered them to bring their brother Benjamin, Jacob's youngest son and now his favorite, back to Egypt to prove their innocence, which they did.

Joseph broke down in tears when he saw his brother Benjamin. But he concocted another scheme to test his brothers further. Judah took the bait and made an impassioned plea to Joseph to free Benjamin. This proved to Joseph that his brothers had indeed changed. He revealed his identity to them and dramatically forgave their betrayal.

The pharaoh allowed Joseph to invite his aged father Jacob and his brothers and their families to come to Egypt during the famine. The pharaoh was grateful to Joseph and granted his family land in Goshen, an area of the delta region of the Nile. Some scholars believe this event has historical roots, perhaps taking place sometime during the seventeenth century B.C. Hyksos invaders had conquered the native Egyptians and set up their own dynasty in the Goshen area. The Hyksos were Semitic people, and were favorably disposed to others of their own ethnic background.

Conclusion. With Joseph's story, we conclude our study of Genesis. Through many dramatic stories, the first book of the Bible reveals God's relationship to the world and to Israel. Our God is a loving creator, but also a just judge. Yahweh, the God of covenant, accepts human weakness and continues to love as a redeemer who is faithful to his word. God works through human events, making good come out of apparent evil and molding people according to the divine will.

These themes apply to our lives as well. The Lord accepts and loves us, even in our sinfulness, and works in our lives in unexpected ways. The Lord is present to us, leading and guiding us. Like Abraham and Sarah, Isaac and Rebekah, Jacob and Rachel, and Joseph, we must be faithful to the living Lord who comes to us in our everyday lives. The Lord will always be faithful to us, giving us life, sharing love, blessing us with many good gifts. This is the message we can take from Genesis.

▪ *focus questions* ▪

1. How much historical value should we give to the stories of our ancestors in faith?

2. Identify the *Amorites*. How does Ur figure into the Abraham story?

3. What are three essential ingredients of faith? Discuss how Abraham exhibited each of them.

4. Give two examples of how the Lord cared for Abraham, thus guaranteeing the fulfillment of the covenant promises.

▪ *journal* ▪

1. Read Genesis 42:1—46:7.
2. Pretend you are Joseph. Write a 300-word speech explaining to your brothers why you acted the way you did in this section of Genesis.

The remains of the patriarchs and matriarchs are enshrined in this mosque in Hebron.

5. What did God promise in the covenant with Abraham? What did Abraham have to do in return?

6. How did Abraham prove his faith?

7. Explain how Isaac prefigures Jesus Christ.

8. How did Abraham establish a land right in Canaan?

9. What are two possible interpretations for the name *Jacob*? How do they fit his character?

10. Discuss the meaning of one of Jacob's meetings with God.

11. What is the meaning of the name *Israel*?

12. "God sometimes works through the evil deeds that people do." Illustrate the truth of this statement by discussing the Joseph story.

13. Discuss some lessons we can take from Genesis about our own relationship with God.

14. *Identify* the following:

Abraham	Isaac	Potiphar
Sarah	Esau	Joseph
Hagar	Jacob	Judah
Ishmael	Rebekah	Benjamin
	Laban	

■ *exercises* ■

1. Check a world almanac or a recent encyclopedia article and write a short report on some aspect of a modern-day Arabic people.

2. Imagine you are Sarah. Compose a diary entry that reveals your feelings toward Hagar and her role in your family.

3. Check a biblical dictionary and research marriage customs and practices in Old Testament times.

4. Reread Jacob's struggle with God (Gn 32:23–32). Describe a time when you wrestled with God or his word. What did you want to do? What did the Lord want you to do? Who won the struggle? What did you feel afterward?

■ *vocabulary* ■

Copy the meaning of these words into the vocabulary section of your journal.

folklore   supplant
prefigure   vista

Prayer Reflection

Psalm 19 is a hymn of praise that celebrates Yahweh as creator of the heavens (especially the sun) and the source of the Law. Quoted here is the first part of the psalm. Imagine our ancestors in the faith — semi-nomads who enjoyed the outdoors, endless horizons, and beautiful vistas under the sky. A day close to nature can refresh our own spirits and turn us to God, the source of all the beauty around us.

> How clearly the sky reveals God's glory!
>   How plainly it shows what he has done!
> Each day announces it to the following day;
>   each night repeats it to the next.
> No speech or words are used,
>   no sound is heard;
> yet their message goes out to all the world
>   and is heard to the ends of the earth.
> God made a home in the sky for the sun;
>   it comes out in the morning like a happy bridegroom,
>   like an athlete eager to run a race.
> It starts at one end of the sky
>   and goes across to the other.
>   Nothing can hide from its heat.
>
> — Psalm 19:1–6 (GNB)

reflection

Find a picture of a beautiful sky that, for you, reveals God's glory. Or describe in your journal the most spectacular sky you ever saw. Use poetic images if you like. Share with a classmate.

resolution

As you leave the house each day during the coming week, look at the sky. Pause for a few minutes and enjoy the changing sky. Thank God for allowing you to live another day to see the glories of creation.

chapter 4

Exodus,
Covenant, Law

"Listen, Israel: Yahweh our God is the one, the only Yahweh. You must love Yahweh your God with all your heart, with all your soul, with all your strength."

— Deuteronomy 6:4–5

One day an unmarried man asked his friend, the father of four, "Why do you love your kids so much?" The father did not hesitate to give his response: "Because they're mine."

This man's children did not have to earn their dad's love; it was theirs unconditionally. The Bible tells us that God's love is like that. God loves us as we are. If we believe this exciting truth of our faith, we will trust and obey God in return.

This message of God's love is clear in the last four books of the Pentateuch — Exodus, Leviticus, Numbers, and Deuteronomy. In them we discover a saving God, a God who chose Israel from among all the nations, rescued it from Egypt, and gave it a land.

Moses reminds the Israelites:

> "Yahweh set his heart on you and chose you not because you were the most numerous of all peoples — for indeed you were the smallest of all — but because he loved you and meant to keep the oath which he swore to your ancestors: that was why Yahweh brought you out with his mighty hand and redeemed you from the place of slave-labor, from the power of Pharaoh king of Egypt" (Dt 7:7–8).

These verses reveal that ours is a God of covenant, a God who keeps the divine promises. The books of Exodus and Numbers tell the dramatic story of God freeing the Chosen People from Egypt, sustaining them for forty years in the desert, and entering into a covenant with them. They also tell us how the people often complained to God and failed to trust God completely. Leviticus and Deuteronomy elaborate the laws God asked the Chosen People to observe in return for the special bond they had entered into.

The Ten Commandments

The heart of Israel's response to God's gracious love was to live the Law. The Ten Commandments summarize the obligations of all who love God. We must respond to God and neighbor. Read Exodus 20:1–17. Reflect on the meaning of each commandment for your life and evaluate how well you are living it right now. Check off the appropriate column: **VW** (doing very well on this); **S** (struggling); **NW** (needs work).

		VW	S	NW
1.	**I am Yahweh your God.... You shall have no other gods to rival me.** God is the top priority in my life. Nothing else has my utmost loyalty — not possessions, power over others, prestige, sex, etc.			
2.	**You shall not misuse the name of Yahweh your God.** I respect God's name and everything else that is holy.			
3.	**Remember the Sabbath day and keep it holy.** I worship God every Sunday. I renew my spirit through rest, healthful activities, and prayer on that day.			
4.	**Honor your father and your mother.** I honor and obey my parents, respect the other members of my family, and listen to others who hold authority over me.			
5.	**You shall not kill.** I respect all life as a gift from God. I refrain from practices that would harm me or others. I show care for those who most need love.			
6.	**You shall not commit adultery.** I respect my own sexuality and that of others. I refrain from doing anything that would bring shame to me as a child of God and a temple of the Holy Spirit.			

	VW	S	NW
7. **You shall not steal.** I am honest in all my dealings, a person of integrity. I do not cheat or steal.			
8. **You shall not give false evidence against your neighbor.** My word is honorable. I always tell the truth. I do not spread gossip or ruin the reputations of others.			
9/10. **You shall not set your heart on your neighbor's house. You shall not set your heart on your neighbor's spouse.** I am not envious over other people's good fortune. I am not jealous. I guard against lust.			

▪ *discuss* ▪

1. Brainstorm to come up with a list of fifteen practices common in today's world that show a lack of respect for life. (Find newspaper and magazine articles that illustrate these practices.)
2. If God asked you to compose three additional commandments for the modern world, what would they be?

▪ *journal* ▪

1. Copy into your journal Deuteronomy's version of the Ten Commandments (Dt 5:1–21). Note several differences in the two versions.
2. Rewrite the commandments in your own words. Turn all negative statements into positive ones.

Historical Background

The Exodus refers to the Israelites' escape from Egypt. It is the foundational event of the Chosen People. Before the Exodus, the stories of our ancestors in the faith centered on individuals or families. But God delivered them from slavery in Egypt, marking the true beginning of their history as a separate *nation*. God uniquely singled out Israel to witness to the one true Lord.

The miracle of the Exodus proved God's love and power. It was sealed in the Sinai covenant where God revealed himself amidst thunder and lightning. Using the prophet Moses as spokesperson, God declared himself bound to his people. God delivered them from slavery, offered protection in the desert, and promised them a land. For their part, the Israelites solemnly promised that they belonged to God, that they were God's special people.

The Sinai covenant helped create the nation of Israel. It revealed the terms of the relationship between God and the Chosen People. Because of God's special intervention on behalf of the Israelites, God expected his people to observe special duties to him and to each other. In short, God wanted the Israelites to distinguish themselves among the nations by keeping the laws set down for them.

The biblical authors recognized in the Exodus experience and the Sinai covenant God's graciousness to the Israelites. For example, when the Priestly author edited Exodus, he was keenly aware of the recent experience of the Jews' captivity in Babylon. Their return to the Promised Land after decades of exile in a foreign country paralleled the first Exodus. The biblical author used the Exodus experience to remind his contemporaries to repent of their sinfulness and keep the Law.

Slavery in Egypt.   The book of Exodus opens around four centuries after the death of Jacob and Joseph. Egypt was comparatively secure economically. The Nile River enabled it to weather famines that periodically struck the ancient Near East. Thus, Egypt attracted nomadic tribes trying to survive the hard times that hit their own lands. Ancient Egyptian records refer to various of these displaced tribes as *'apiru*. Ancestors of the Israelites probably intermarried with some of these other Semitic tribes. The word *Hebrew* comes from this Egyptian word *'apiru*.

Around 1500 B.C. the native Egyptians overthrew the Hyksos. Under a series of new kings, Egypt's power in the Near East grew enormously. In general, these kings tightened the reins on foreign inhabitants in Egypt. In most cases they reduced them to slaves who had to work on extensive building projects.

Pharaoh Akhenaton (1375–1358 B.C.), one of these new kings, attempted to establish monotheism in Egypt. Egyptians worshiped many gods, but a special place was reserved for *Ra*, the sun god who created humans. The other important Egyptian god was *Osiris*, the god of the underworld. When Akhenaton came to power, he promoted the worship of *Aton* (the sun disc) as the only supreme god in the universe. Some scholars believe the monotheism of the Egyptians helped the Israelites solidify their own monotheistic faith in Yahweh.

The Pharaoh of the Exodus. Most scholars agree that the Exodus took place in the thirteenth century B.C., probably during the reign of Ramses II, a great builder who ruled between 1290 to 1224 B.C. Egyptian records show that he used *'apiru* in his various building projects, including the cities of Pithom and Ramses. Although no one knows for certain the exact year of the Exodus event itself, many scholars suggest that it took place around 1250 B.C. Egyptian historical records take no notice of some *'apiru* who decided to flee Egypt. Various tribes leaving to return to their own lands could have been a common occurrence. However, for the Chosen People, their flight from Egypt and God's part in it made all the difference in the world.

Reading Exodus (please read Ex 1—4; 12—14). Exodus was composed by three people — the Yahwist who wrote in the tenth century B.C. during the time of Solomon and David; the Elohist who wrote in the eighth century, probably from the northern kingdom; and the Priestly writer who wrote after the Exile in the sixth century.

The hero of Exodus is Moses, who is the great servant of God. He is the model for other servants in the Bible: Joshua, Jeremiah, Second Isaiah, and Jesus. Himself a Hebrew, Moses shared the plight of his people. He was close to God and served as a mediator between God and the Chosen People. Again and again he called the Israelites to be faithful to the God who was accomplishing such great things for them.

Outline of Exodus

1. The Flight from Egypt 1:1—15:21
2. Israel in the desert 15:22—18:27
3. The Sinai covenant 19:1—24:17
4. Instructions about the Tabernacle 25:1—40:38

Moses

Exodus begins by reporting how the fortunes of the Israelites had changed since the time of Joseph. The new pharaohs enslaved them and even tried to suppress them by killing the baby boys. Instead of a decrease in population, however, the Israelites grew in number.

Birth of Moses.   During this crisis the prophet Moses was born. The stories of his birth — his floating down the river, and his rescue by an Egyptian princess — closely parallel the literature of the ancient Akkadians. King Sargon (around 2300 B.C.) was also saved after being put in basket of rushes and cast into a river. The pharaoh's daughter adopted Moses, a name meaning "draw out," and unknowingly employed Moses' own mother as his nurse. Thus, Moses knew his true identity as an Israelite, but he grew up as Egyptian royalty.

Flight to Midian.   Moses had to flee Egypt when, in anger, he killed an Egyptian overlord for attacking one of his Hebrew kinsmen. Moses' period of exile in the Sinai desert among the Midianites prepared him to lead the Israelites through the barren desert. Moses lived among the desert people for many years as a shepherd. He married and fathered a son named Gershom, meaning "stranger in a foreign land."

Burning Bush.   One day, while tending his sheep, Moses saw an amazing vision: a burning bush that did not burn itself out. Moses moved closer to examine this wondrous curiosity. As he approached the bush he heard God call out, instructing him to remove his sandals. The ground Moses stood on was holy because of God's presence.

God instructed Moses to return to Egypt to lead the Chosen People to freedom. Moses complained that he was incapable of handling such a mission. But the Lord assured Moses of his help and even revealed the divine name to him, *Yahweh.* In so doing, the Lord entered into an intimate relationship with Moses. He assured him that *I AM* was the "God of Abraham, the God of Isaac, the God of Jacob" who had always cared for his special people.

Again Moses protested. How could he, a simple shepherd, speak convincingly to his enslaved people? Through graphic signs — changing Moses' staff into a serpent and making Moses' hand appear leprous — God promised Moses that a divine power would be with him. When Moses objected that he was slow of speech and thus inadequate for God's appointed role for him, God also appointed Aaron as a spokes-man for Moses.

Back to Egypt. Moses and Aaron returned to Egypt and convinced the Israelites that God had indeed heard their prayers for deliverance. Moses easily convinced the Israelites that God had chosen them. However, convincing the pharaoh that he should free the Israelites proved more difficult. Rather than free the Israelites from their slavery, the pharaoh doubled their work load. The Israelites turned on Moses. He had not delivered on his promises, and it looked like God had abandoned them.

Ten Plagues. Exodus 7—12:30 tells of the famous ten plagues of Egypt. This story of the plagues stresses the pharaoh's hardness of heart and the Lord's power to help the Chosen People.

The plague stories contain the following elements: Moses requests that the pharaoh free the Israelites; the pharaoh refuses; the Lord punishes the Egyptians with a plague; the pharaoh begs Moses to bring relief from the disaster; the Lord honors Moses' request to stop the plague; the pharaoh refuses, after a plague's respite, to honor his word.

The ten plagues were:

1. Bloody water (7:17)
2. Frogs (8:2)
3. Gnats (8:13)
4. Flies (8:20)
5. Pestilence on the livestock (9:3)
6. Boils (9:10)
7. Hail (9:23)
8. Locusts (10:13)
9. Darkness over the land (10:22)
10. Death of the firstborn (11:5)

How are we to interpret the plagues — miracles or common phenomena? Various commentators have suggested natural explanations for the plagues. For example, the reddening of the Nile was not blood but the clogging of the river by red silt. When the Nile receded, it often left frogs in its wake. Decaying frogs would bring gnats and flies, which spread disease to both cattle and people. Hail, locusts, and blinding sandstorms that blotted out the sun were also known in ancient Egypt.

Other interpreters claim that a comet may have hit the earth causing red dust, earthquakes, and other disastrous effects. Or perhaps a volcano erupted and brought a tidal wave that led to natural disasters and the plagues.

We can never really know what happened because Exodus does not give scientific data about ancient events. The literary style of Exodus is folklore. The popular stories teach one important truth: Yahweh, more powerful than any earthly king, brought the Chosen People out of Egypt.

■

Being Hard of Heart

Exodus repeatedly tells us that the pharaoh's heart was hardened (7:13, 14, 22; 8:15; 9:7, 35); or that he hardened his own heart (8:11, 28); or that the Lord hardened pharaoh's heart (7:3; 9:12; 10:1, 20, 27). Read these passages.

■ *discuss* ■

1. Who is in control here — God or the pharaoh?
2. How does the pharaoh show that he thinks *he* is in control?
3. Discuss some reasons God might have hardened the pharaoh's heart.

■

■ *journal* ■

Write of a time when your own pride led to your being punished.

Passover.   The tenth plague was the most severe of all. It is commemorated by Israel's most important religious feast, the Passover. On the night of the fourteenth day of Nisan (corresponding to our March or April), each Israelite family was to slay and roast a young lamb and smear its blood on the door-posts and lintel of the house.

The Israelites were to eat the lamb quickly with unleavened bread — yeasted bread would take too long to rise — and bitter herbs. The blood from the lamb, smeared on the doors signaled the Lord's avenging angel to pass over the Hebrew homes on its mission to strike down the firstborn of the Egyptians.

Yahweh instructed Israel to celebrate this meal every year to remind future generations of God's deliverance, salvation, fidelity, and love. Yahweh's Passover struck fear into the Egyptian people and their pharaoh, who finally allowed the Hebrews to leave.

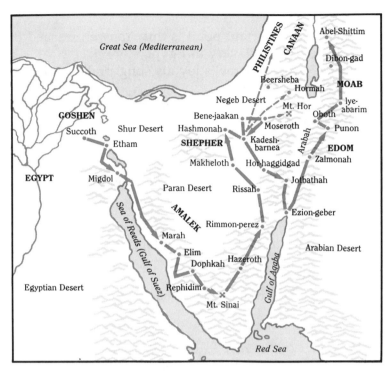

The map shows locations including: Great Sea (Mediterranean), GOSHEN, Succoth, Shur Desert, Hashmonah, SHEPHER, Makheloth, Paran Desert, Rissah, AMALEK, Marah, Elim, Dophkah, Hazeroth, Rephidim, Mt. Sinai, Egyptian Desert, EGYPT, Migdol, Etham, Sea of Reeds (Gulf of Suez), Gulf of Aqaba, Red Sea, Rimmon-perez, Ezion-geber, Arabian Desert, Jotbathah, Zalmonah, EDOM, Punon, Oboth, Kadesh-barnea, Hor-haggidgad, Bene-jaakan, Moseroth, Mt. Hor, Negeb Desert, Beersheba, Hormah, PHILISTINES, CANAAN, Abel-Shittim, Dibon-gad, MOAB, Iye-abarim, Arabah

Exodus to Freedom

The Israelites had spent 430 years in Egypt (Ex 12:40). Finally, they were free to go, but God did not lead them via the shortest route, through Philistine territory, "'in case,' God thought, 'the prospect of fighting makes the people change their minds and turn back to Egypt'" (Ex 13:17). Rather, in a pillar of cloud by day and fire by night, the Lord led the people through the Reed (Red) Sea, a marshy area near the present-day Suez Canal.

The Egyptians regretted freeing the slaves and hotly pursued them in their chariots. But the Lord "so clogged their chariot wheels that they drove on only with difficulty" (14:25). The Israelites feared the pharaoh and complained to Moses that they should have remained in Egypt as slaves. However, in a mighty gesture symbolizing God's power, Moses stretched out his hand and the waters surged back to drown the pursuing Egyptians.

Did this all take place as depicted in Exodus? Was the sea parted so the Israelites could escape? Did Moses perform a spectacular miracle to save his people? We do not know. Perhaps hot winds dried the marshy swamps so the Israelites could pass and, later, tidal waves drowned the

Egyptians. The important point is this: Yahweh rescued the Chosen People from slavery in Egypt.

Exodus 15 records Israel's joyous song praising God for the wondrous victory:

It was then that Moses and the Israelites sang this song in Yahweh's honor:

> I shall sing to Yahweh, for he has covered himself in
>   glory,
>   horse and rider he has thrown into the sea.
> Yah is my strength and my song,
> to him I owe my deliverance.
> He is my God and I shall praise him,
> my father's God and I shall extol him.
> Yahweh is a warrior;
> Yahweh is his name.
>
> Pharaoh's chariots and army he has hurled into the sea
>   (Ex 15:1—4a).

In the Desert (please read Ex 16—18). The Chosen People are now moving from the Reed Sea to Mount Sinai. Along the way, the Israelites grumbled about their hardships in the desert. God tested them, but also responded to their needs. Moses freshened bitter waters and brought forth water from a rock to quench their thirst. To satisfy their hunger, God sent quail and manna (a sweet edible substance secreted by the tamarisk tree). With the help of Moses' raised arms, symbolizing God's might, Joshua defeated the Amalekites who tried to destroy them. Finally, heeding the advice of his father-in-law, Jethro, Moses assigned able leaders to handle disputes as they arose during the journey.

How many people journeyed in the desert? The Bible tells us 600,000 Israelites fled Egypt, but the biblical authors, writing during King David's glory days, exaggerated this number. Probably no more than a few hundred or thousand Israelite slaves fled Egypt. From this group of fleeing refugees, God would create the nation of Israel, a special people.

When they finally came to Mount Sinai, Moses spoke on God's behalf:

> "You have seen for yourselves what I did to the Egyptians and how I carried you away on eagle's wings and brought you to me. So now, if you are really prepared to obey me and keep my covenant, you, out of all peoples, shall be my personal possession, for the whole world is

■ *reading* ■

Read Ex 19—24; 32—33 and answer the following questions in your journal.

1. Describe some key elements of the *theophany* (appearance of God) on Mount Sinai.
2. What three feasts must Israelites celebrate each year (23:14–17)?
3. Why did the people make the golden calf? Why did Moses break the stone tablets (Ex 32)?
4. Describe the relationship between God and Moses (Ex 33:7–23).

mine. For me you shall be a kingdom of priests, a holy nation" (Ex 19:4b–6).

Covenant

Now at daybreak two days later, there were peals of thunder and flashes of lightning, dense cloud on the mountain and a very loud trumpet blast; and, in the camp, all the people trembled (Ex 19:16).

With these words Exodus introduces Yahweh's remarkable meeting with Moses and the Israelites on Mount Sinai. God spoke to Moses and made a covenant with the Israelites; from now on, the Israelites would be *God's chosen people*, a holy nation especially blessed by God. An excellent summary of the covenant can be found in Exodus 34:6:

Yahweh, Yahweh, God of tenderness and compassion, slow to anger, rich in faithful love and constancy, maintaining his faithful love to thousands, forgiving fault, crime and sin, yet letting nothing go unchecked.

Later, the prophets came to express the covenant in this simple formula: "You shall be my people and I will be your God" (Jer 7:23, Ez 11:20, Hos 2:25).

God's freely chosen covenant is the heart of the religion of the Israelites.

- It bound God and the Chosen People in a personal, loving union.
- It revealed God's special love and mercy for them.
- It stipulated how God's people were to respond to his love and uphold their part of the covenant. First, they must follow the commandments. Second, they must be faithful to God through obedience and worship.

The various biblical authors (J, E, and P) overlap different details in their reports of the Sinai covenant. However, they agree that: 1) God visited the Israelites in an overpowering theophany (manifestation of divine power); 2) God expressed the divine will for his people; and 3) Moses reported the will of God. He was the mediator of the covenant, God's spokesperson.

Sealing of the Covenant. Israel accepted the divine will. "All the words Yahweh has spoken we will carry out!" (Ex

24:3). Moses put into writing all the Lord taught him and sealed the covenant by building an altar with twelve pillars (to represent the twelve tribes). He killed some young bulls and splashed their blood on the altar (a symbol of God) and on the people. Blood represented life. Through Moses' ritual action, Yahweh and the Israelites joined in a common life, sealing their destiny for all time.

Ten Commandments.   Exodus 20—23 summarizes the divinely revealed moral duties the Chosen People must keep. The Ten Commandments (20:1–17) provide an excellent summary of what later came to be called the Law. They imitate in rough form the ancient covenants that kings made with their subjects.

1. First is a *preamble* (in which God gives his name) and a *historical prologue* in which God reviews his past acts of kindness to the people.

2. Next are the *stipulations or demands* that God imposes on his people. The first three commandments stress the obligation to put God above everything. The next seven command us to love neighbor as self.

3. The carving of the commandments on stone corresponds to the *depositing* of the ancient covenants in temples and their periodic public reading.

4. Finally, a covenant typically concluded with *curses and blessings* and a call to *divine witnesses*. The Sinai covenant, unlike covenants that called upon the gods as witnesses, has Yahweh, who is God alone, as party to the contract itself. There is no need for further divine witness.

The Law.   The Israelites agreed to live a new life in conformity with God's will, using the Ten Commandments as their basic guide. For the Israelites, the commandments were the heart of the Law. Over the years, Israel added many laws to the basic ten to help the people adapt to new situations of worshiping God and treating others justly.

The books of Exodus, Leviticus, Numbers, and Deuteronomy contain 613 laws. Some of these appear strange and even barbaric to us today. Usually, Israel's laws reflected a major moral advance over those of neighboring peoples. Scholars have shown us similarities between Israel's laws and those of other peoples of the time, such as the famous Babylonian Code of Hammurabi (c. 1700 B.C.). Israel reshaped these borrowed laws to support its belief in Yahweh, the one God who rescued and sustained the Chosen People.

The biblical authors attributed laws made much later to Moses, the first law-giver. These later laws grew out of the Mosaic foundations. Many of them were attempts to reform the Israelites and ignite the original spark of enthusiasm for the covenant at Sinai.

For example, scholars agree that the whole book of Deuteronomy, a term meaning "second law," was a restatement and further development of Mosaic law. Deuteronomy resulted from a reform movement that began in the northern kingdom shortly before its conquest. It reflects the concerns of the prophets who constantly had to remind the people and their leaders to be single-hearted in their devotion to the covenant.

The Golden Calf.   Most of the remainder of Exodus gives instructions for building the ark of the covenant, which would contain the Law tablets, and the Tabernacle, or sacred tent, in which God would meet Moses. The Tabernacle would be the symbol of God's abiding presence with his people.

However, the people were impatient with Moses and his long meetings with God on the mountain. With Aaron's help, they decided to build their own symbol of god — a golden calf or young bull. Their own pride caused them to form Yahweh in the image of the gods of their neighbors, and to worship the image itself rather than worshiping God alone.

Covenant Renewed.   Moses intervened with Yahweh on behalf of the people to prevent divine wrath from destroying them for the worst breach of the covenant — worshiping false gods. He descended from the mountain and, blazing with anger, threw down and broke the tablets of the Law to symbolize the people's transgression. Moses angrily reproached Aaron, put many of the false worshipers to death, and returned to the mountain to beg God's forgiveness.

Moved by Moses' appeals, Yahweh agreed to renew the covenant and remain with the Chosen People. Yahweh passed before Moses and called out, revealing his identity (cf. Ex 34:6–7). The Lord once again wrote the words of the covenant on new tablets, thus renewing the covenant with the people. The Lord proved loyal to the unfaithful people and even promised:

"I shall work such wonders at the head of your whole people as have never been worked in any other country or nation, and all the people round you will see what Yahweh can do, for what I shall do through you will be awe-inspiring" (Ex 34:10).

Moses descended from the mountain, his face shining with God's glory. The Lord would remain with the Israelites as they marched to the Promised Land, a journey described in the book of Numbers.

▪ *discuss* ▪

1. How are people unfaithful to God in today's world? What are the "golden calves" our contemporary world worships?
2. Reread Ex 33:12–23. What kind of man must Moses have been?

▪ *journal* ▪

Study Ex 34:6–7. Which trait of God most impresses you? Which quality most surprises you? Explain your answer. (Note: At the time of Exodus' writing, the Israelites did not have a clear idea of life after death. If their sins in this life went unrepented and unpunished, they believed their families would suffer the results of their iniquities.)

Leviticus

▪ *discuss* ▪

Leviticus 1 gives laws about sacrifices in which the entire animal (except its hide) was burned on the altar. The holocaust, offered in praise, symbolized total giving to God.

What is the significance of the 20th-century term *Holocaust*, referring to the experience of the Jews in Nazi Germany?

The book of Leviticus derives its name from the priests of the tribe of Levi who were in charge of Israel's official worship. Many of its 247 laws regulate public worship, animal sacrifices, and ritual offerings. Other laws govern the behavior of priests and give directions for the celebration of religious feasts.

Composed by the Priestly author, Leviticus' main teaching is that God is holy. This theme of holiness permeates Leviticus. God is the source of all life, the divine being worthy of our utmost attention and adoration. Everything associated with God — especially priests and places and ways of worship — are also holy.

God's people are holy, too, because God has especially chosen them. Holiness in us means respect for the sacredness of life and God's presence in ordinary life. Leviticus taught the Chosen People to be holy by including laws that govern all aspects of human life, including sex, birth, diseases, and death. All these participate in a special way in God's creative action in the world. They are part of the mystery of life which is under God's control.

Outline of Leviticus

Lv 1—7:	kinds of sacrifice: holocausts (burnt offerings); grain, peace, sin, and guilt offerings; directions for performing sacrifices
Lv 8—10:	the appointment of Aaron and his descendants as Israel's true priesthood
Lv 11—15:	uncleanness associated with living beings
Lv 16:	the ritual Day of Atonement
Lv 17—26:	"The Law of Holiness" — ethical and social obligations of a holy people who try to live a godly life

Sampling Leviticus

Read Leviticus 16.

- *Day of Atonement* Yom Kippur (Hebrew for "Day of Atonement") purified the Israelites and their land of sins and transgressions committed the previous year. The ritual of the scapegoat (16:20–28) transferred the sins of the people to the animal. A man led the goat to the desert, believed to be the home of satan, to die of thirst and starvation. With the animal's death, the people's sins returned to the evil spirits and their guilt was taken away.

  Modern-day Jews celebrate Yom Kippur on the ninth day of their New Year (September-October). Christians believe that Jesus became a voluntary scapegoat who took on the sins of all humanity. His sacrifice on the cross relieved humanity of the burden of sin, made us one with God, and won eternal life for us.

Read Leviticus 25:1–22.

- *Sabbatical/Jubilee years.* The sabbatical year rested the soil. It called for faith in God to provide for his people during the year the soil lay fallow. The owner could harvest any growth that sprang up from the previous year's plantings. The poor could also take what they needed.

The Jubilee year had both religious and social justice purposes. By freeing slaves every fifty years, the Israelites recalled their own liberation from slavery. By returning property to its original owners, the Chosen People recognized their dependence on God who was the true owner of the land. And, again, the poor had the right to take the aftergrowth or pick grapes from the untended vines.

Numbers

The book of Numbers gets its name from the many lists it contains — lists of tribes, leaders, march formations, offerings, and two censuses of the Israelites as they marched from Mount Sinai to the plains of Moab across from Jericho. The Hebrew title of the book is "in the wilderness," which is a fitting name. Numbers describes the period between the thirteen months after the Exodus and the end of the forty years of wandering in the Sinai desert.

The Priestly author predominates in Numbers 1—10, 15—19, and 26—36. His main interests are the Tabernacle, sacrifice, and regulations for worship. He is also concerned with genealogies, lists, and chronologies. An editor (JE) combined the basic narrative structure in Numbers 10—25, drawing on the Yahwist and Elohist traditions.

The first of two major themes is Yahweh's care for the Chosen People. The Lord led them with a cloud by day and fire by night. He listened to Moses' pleas for the people, providing food, water, and military victory. His glorious presence, symbolized by a cloud, hung over the ark of the covenant, a wooden chest that held the tablets of the Law. Never did the Lord withdraw his promises of devotion to the people.

The second theme concerns the constant "murmuring" of the Hebrews — complaints, discontentment, and even rebellion against God's chosen leader, Moses. For example, the Israelites complained about the food that God gave them (Nm 11). When Moses' sister, Miriam, and brother, Aaron, criticized Moses' leadership, their jealousy led to Miriam's suffering a leprous condition for a week (Nm 12).

A key example of this murmuring occurred when Israelite spies reported disheartening news about the ferocity and size of the Canaanites. The people despaired of the Lord's ability to save them. They wanted to return to Egypt and no longer trusted Moses' leadership. God remained faithful to the covenant, but still punished the people by making them wander in the desert for forty years before entering the "land flowing with milk and honey." Furthermore, the Lord would not permit anyone of the first generation to enter the Promised Land except Caleb and Joshua who had counseled the Israelites to believe in God's promises (Nm 13–14).

Moses himself faltered at Meribah, turning a manifestation of God's power in bringing water from the rock into a chance to express his anger toward the people for their lack of faith. Because of their infidelity, God did not permit either Aaron or Moses to lead the people into the Promised Land (Nm 20).

Numbers tells us about the many infidelities of the Israelites. Their lack of faith, disobedience, and rebellious attitude brought about punishment. For example, the disobedient generation died before seeing the Promised Land. Human sin has its consequences. But God remained faithful to his word. Numbers ends with the Israelites on the threshold of the Promised Land.

Numbers' Lessons. We can apply the truth taught in the Book of Numbers to our own lives: We may sin; we may misuse and even fear our freedom; we may doubt God's presence with us; our sins may deserve punishment. However, Numbers teaches that God is faithful to us throughout our earthly journey.

Outline of Numbers

1. Nm 1:1—10:10
   - organization of Israel before leaving Mount Sinai

2. Nm 10:11—21:25
   - the desert march from Sinai to the plains of Moab

3. Nm 22:1—36:13
   - preparing for entry into the Promised Land

■

Sampling Numbers

Read Nm 22—24.

Balaam and his oracles. Scholars attribute the Balaam stories to the Yahwist and Elohist authors. Balaam was a seer widely known in many ancient Near Eastern cultures. In this story, the Israelites had reached the borders of Canaan on the plains of Moab. The Moabites, descendants of Lot's incestuous relationship with his daughter (Gn 19:30–38), lived here. Balak, their king, feared the Israelites. Thus, he sent for Balaam and offered to pay him to curse the Israelites.

Ancient people believed that a prophet's blessing or curse would take place. But God had other plans. Balaam ended up blessing, not cursing, the Chosen People. No one can thwart God's plans. The Lord will use the most unlikely sources to accomplish the divine will.

1. What is the point of the "talking ass" in 22:23–35?

2. Cite two references that show Balaam's faith in Yahweh.

3. Why can't Balaam curse the Israelites?

4. To what animals does Balaam compare Israel (23:24; 24:8, 9)?

5. Check your Bible's footnote to 24:17. To whom does it apply this verse?

Deuteronomy

Deuteronomy has several features that distinguish it from the other books of the Pentateuch.

Composition.   Although it claims to be from the time of Moses, it really comes from a later period. Scholars believe its traditions date from about the seventh century B.C., near the end of Israel's time as an independent kingdom. Some northern Levite reformers, moved by the message of prophets like Elijah, Amos, and Hosea, wrote a second edition of the Law to update it and apply it to Israel's changed situation. When the city of Samaria, the capital of the northern kingdom, fell in 721 B.C., these reformers moved to Jerusalem and completed their work there.

The reforms did not catch on at first because corrupt kings such as Manasseh suppressed the book. King Josiah (640–609 B.C.), however, sought to reform the faith of the people who had drifted away from the covenant. 2 Kings 22—23 tells the story of the rediscovery of Deuteronomy during Josiah's reign and his great desire to teach it to the people.

The final editing of Deuteronomy, like all the books of the Pentateuch, took place after the Exile.

Literary Style.   Unlike the other books of the Pentateuch, Deuteronomy is in the form of three heartfelt and emotional sermons preached by Moses to the second-generation Israelites before they entered the Promised Land at the end of the forty years in the desert. The title of the book translates as "second law," but it means a repetition of the Law for the new generation of Israelites, not a new law.

The book's real audience was later generations of Israelites who needed encouragement to respond anew and wholeheartedly to God and the covenant. Deuteronomy is an impassioned plea to live the Law by worshiping Yahweh and extending God's love and justice to the poor and needy.

Theological Themes.   The theology of Deuteronomy centers around God's love of Israel and unhappiness with the people for worshiping false gods and not responding wholeheartedly to his love. The book also teaches that discipline is a sign of God's love, and it exhorts Israel to make a choice between the way of obedience to God and the Law (life) and the way of disobedience (death).

Outline of Deuteronomy

1—4	first address describing the journey from Mount Horeb (Sinai) to Moab
5—11	second address introducing the book of Law
12—26	the Law book
27—34	third address — Moses' last will and testament; death of Moses

■

Sampling Deuteronomy

1. A central theme in Deuteronomy is the system of rewards and punishments for obeying or disobeying God. Read Deuteronomy 8:1–20; 11:8–17, 26–28; 28:1–69 and record answers to the following questions in your journal.

- What is obedience? What blessings follow obedience?
- What is disobedience? What curses follow disobedience?

2. Read the following passages. Answer the questions.

Proofs of God's love (4:32–40).
Why did God do all the marvels he did for Israel?

Shema, Israel (6:4–9).
This prayer (meaning "Listen, Israel") is the heart of the Jewish faith. Memorize it. Some Jews write the words of this prayer (see also Dt 11:13–21 and Nm 15:37–41) on a parchment scroll (called a *mezuzah*) and then fasten it to the doorposts of their houses. Others place the words in small leather boxes (*phylacteries*) worn on the left arm and forehead when praying. Thus, God's word is close to one's mind and heart.

God's care (8:1–20).
Why did God test the Israelites (8:1–5)?

What is the danger of too much prosperity?

■ *discuss* ■

Read Mt 4:1–11, an account of Jesus' temptations in the desert. Note the references your Bible gives to Deuteronomy (8:2,3; 6:16; 34:1–4; 6:13). What might Jesus have been tempted to do in his earthly ministry? What were some major temptations of Israel?

Love (10:12–22).
Deuteronomy underscores time and again God's love for the Israelites. List five traits of this loving God.

Prophet (18:9–22).
What is a major sign of a true prophet?
To whom might this passage refer?

Social justice (24:10–22).
What attitude should we have toward the poor and defenseless?

Thanksgiving (26:1–11).
These verses state the faith of the Israelites (creed), vv. 6–10. Why should the Chosen People thank God?

Moses' death (34:1–12).
What is the last thing Moses sees before his death?

—————————————— ■ ——————————————

The Pentateuch continuously speaks of God's love, the covenant he made with the Israelites. Christians believe God completed this covenant with us through Jesus. We, like Israel, are undeserving of God's love. We, like Israel, have experienced an exodus — a rescue from sin and death by Jesus' passion, death, and resurrection. And we, like Israel, are still on our journey to the promised land of salvation. The Lord has provided food for the journey — the eucharist — and given us a glimpse of what is in store for us.

Deuteronomy reminds us, though, that we, like Israel, travel as a people. We journey not by ourselves but in community with others. We must look out for our fellow pilgrims along the way, especially those who are helpless, poor, and hurting. If we ignore them, we show ingratitude to a God who loves us and saves us.

■ *focus questions* ■

1. Explain why the Exodus experience is the central event of Jewish history.
2. Who was the pharaoh of the Exodus?
3. Discuss three outstanding qualities of Moses.

4. What is a natural explanation for the ten plagues and the parting of the Reed Sea? What is the supernatural explanation for these events?

5. What were the ten plagues of Egypt?

6. Discuss the meaning of the Passover.

7. Discuss several reasons the Israelites "murmured" in the desert. How did God react to this?

8. What is the Sinai covenant? Discuss its significance for the Jewish people.

9. What are the major elements in a typical covenant of the ancient world?

10. List the Ten Commandments from memory. What does each commandment teach?

11. What role did the Law play in the faith of Israel?

12. Discuss several qualities of the God revealed in the last four books of the Pentateuch.

13. Discuss the major theme of Leviticus.

14. Cite and discuss a law that depicts Yahweh's compassion for the poor.

15. Discuss one major theme of Numbers.

16. What is significant about the Balaam stories?

17. What is the literal meaning of the term *Deuteronomy*? Why is this an appropriate name for this biblical book?

18. What are some major themes of Deuteronomy?

19. Identify and discuss the significance of:

'Apiru (Hebrew)   Jubilee year
Pharaoh Akhenaton   Moabites
Balak   Midianites
Josiah   Yom Kippur
sabbatical year   *Shema*

▪ *exercises* ▪

1. Write a short character sketch of the Moses you met in the last four books of the Pentateuch. Use specific biblical passages to help show his character.

2. Read Ex 23:14–17 which describes the requirement to observe the religious feasts of Passover, Pentecost, and Tabernacles. Using a biblical dictionary or a book on Judaism, prepare a report on one of these feasts.

(handwritten margin notes:)
Moses Rahab
Aaron Ai
Caleb
Miriam
Balaam
Achan
Meribah
Kadesh - Barnea
Jericho
Mt Sinai
Mt Hor
Moab
Mt Nebo

the ban
"herem"

▪ *vocabulary* ▪

3. Prepare a report on one of the pyramids and their role in Egyptian religion.

4. Write an imaginary dialogue between God and Moses in which Moses tries to convince God not to destroy the disobedient Israelites. Use humor if you wish.

■

Prayer Reflection

Numbers contains Moses' instructions to Aaron and the priests on how to bless the Chosen People. A blessing conveys prosperity and well-being on another. To receive God's blessing greatly honors us, underscoring our dignity as God's children.

Savor the words of this familiar blessing:

> May Yahweh bless you and keep you.
> May Yahweh let his face shine on you and be gracious
>   to you.
> May Yahweh show you his face and bring you peace.
>
> — Numbers 6:24–26

■ *reflection* ■

How has God shown his face to you? Who, in your life, has best shown you what God is like?

■ *resolution* ■

You, too, can be a living blessing to others. Think of several people who need your smile, good cheer, and love. Do something special for these people during the coming weeks.

■

chapter 5

A Land and a King

"Yahweh Sabaoth says this: I took you from the pasture, from following the sheep, to be leader of my people Israel; I have been with you wherever you went; I have got rid of all your enemies for you. I am going to make your fame as great as the fame of the greatest on earth. I am going to provide a place for my people Israel; I shall plant them there, and there they will live and never be disturbed again.... Yahweh furthermore tells you that he will make you a dynasty.... Your dynasty and your sovereignty will ever stand firm before me and your throne be for ever secure."

— 2 Samuel 7:8–11; 16

Friendship makes our lives worth living. However, what is true friendship and what disguises as friendship? Someone once remarked that false friends are like your shadow. While there is sunshine, they are close by, but the minute you step into the shade, they disappear.

The Native Americans understood what true friends are like. Their word for friend reveals the essence of this special relationship, "one-who-carries-my-sorrow-on-his-back."

The books we will study in this chapter report how God remained firm in his friendship with the Chosen People. The Lord led them into the Promised Land and provided leaders to help them settle there. The Lord also defended them against their enemies, corrected them when they sinned, and gave them a strong king.

These books contain many marvelous stories, among them the accounts of two inspiring friendships: Ruth and her mother-in-law Naomi, and David and Jonathan. In the first case, the widow Ruth left her own country to accompany Naomi back to Israel to comfort and support her. God blessed Ruth's self-sacrifice. She, a foreigner, would become the great-grandmother of King David and, thus, an ancestor of Jesus, the Messiah.

In the second case, Jonathan renounced his claim to his father Saul's throne in favor of his friend David. He perfectly exemplified deep, compassionate friendship-love for David. The Bible records the events of salvation history, but it also shares with us the lives and loves of real flesh-and-blood people. They reach out across the centuries to inspire and instruct us.

Friendship

Part 1 — What kind of friend are you?

Write the initials of your best friend here: _____. Now, read the following traits or qualities of friendship taught in the Bible. Judge how well you exhibit each of these in your relationship to your best friend.

VT = very true of me; **T** = true of me; **NT** = not true of me.

	VT	T	NT
1. **Self-sacrificing**: "Whatever you think best, I will certainly do for you" (1 Sm 20:4).			
2. **Confidentiality**: "The trustworthy keeps things hidden" (Prv 11:13b).			
3. **Dependability**: "A friend is a friend at all times" (Prv 17:17a).			
4. **Compassionate**: "The sweetness of friendship rather than self-reliance" (Prv 27:9b).			
5. **Humble**: "Give preference to others, everyone pursuing not selfish interests but those of others" (Phil 2:4a).			
6. **Positive influence**: "There are friends who point the way to ruin, others are closer than a brother" (Prv 18:24).			

Part 2: Here is a list of twelve traits people might look for in a friend. Check off four that you feel are the most important for *your* friends to have.

- [ ] intelligent
- [ ] attractive
- [ ] lots of personality
- [ ] honest
- [ ] generous
- [ ] kind
- [ ] rich
- [ ] good listener
- [ ] athletic
- [ ] sense of humor
- [ ] morally upright
- [ ] loyal

■ *discuss* ■

1. What is the *most important* quality of friendship? Why?

2. Give examples of "friends who point the way to ruin." How can you, in a practical way, cope with these kinds of friends?

■ *journal* ■

Read Colossians 3:12–14. Write an essay explaining how you demonstrated to a close friend three traits mentioned in this passage.

Joshua and Judges

The books of Joshua and Judges span the time from the death of Moses to the beginning of the monarchy, roughly from 1250 to 1030 B.C. They describe the Israelites' move into and settlement of the Promised Land and their relationship to the various Canaanite tribes living there. The theological concerns are the same as those found in the book of Deuteronomy.

These books give two different accounts of how the Chosen People conquered the Promised Land. The book of Joshua gives the impression that the conquest was swift and sure. Composed several centuries after the conquest, Joshua gives an idealized picture in order to convey its major theological theme: Yahweh fought for Israel; Israel did not act on its own; without the Lord's help, the miracle of settling in the "land flowing with milk and honey" would never have taken place.

The book of Judges, on the other hand, reports a series of bitter struggles against the Canaanites, contests that spanned a period of around two hundred years. Archaeology supports the book of Joshua's assertion that several major battles gave the Israelites strategic footholds in the land and a basis for later expansion. However, Judges shows what a lengthy struggle this conquest actually was.

Politically, the tribes that settled in Canaan (Israel) were a confederacy, loosely held together by their religious allegiance to Yahweh. Various of these tribes made gains in Canaan through infiltration and assimilation of earlier inhabitants. But the native population also threatened to assimilate or destroy the Israelites.

Outline of Joshua

1. Time of preparation (1:1—2:24)
2. Entrance into the land (3:1—5:15)
3. Conquest of the Promised Land (6:1—12:24)
4. Division of the land (13:1—21:45)
5. Joshua's farewell and covenant renewal (22:1—24:33)

▪ *reading* ▪

Read Joshua 1—3; 9—10; 24. Answer the questions in your journal.

1. How is Joshua like Moses?
2. How did the Gibeonites save themselves? (Ch. 9)
3. What symbolized Joshua's renewal of the covenant?

Judges shows how the patriarchal system that kept Israel alive in the desert began to break down after Joshua's death. The tribes often ignored the covenant, which required that they worship the one true God — Yahweh. They turned to the worship of the native gods of the Canaanites. The Israelites also had many enemies to contend with in this period besides the Canaanites.

During these troubled times God remained with the Israelites even when they turned from him. The spirit of the Lord descended on certain tribal rulers called *judges* who helped deliver the people from their oppressors. These judges were not primarily legal arbiters as in the modern sense of the word. Rather, they were chieftains of tribes and were known for their military prowess. The Lord empowered them to organize several tribes to conquer Israel's enemies.

We find in Judges the constant theme of the Deuteronomist historian: although God punished the Israelites for their faithlessness, he also listened to their cries for help. The Lord remained with them by raising military heroes who saved Israel until the time when a strong leader, a king, would unite all the tribes into a single nation. God was faithful to the covenant, even though the Israelites were not.

Joshua.   The book of Joshua picks up where Deuteronomy left off. It describes how the Lord helped the Israelites conquer the land of Canaan and fulfilled the promise made to Abraham. This work takes its name from Joshua, the ideal military hero who figured prominently in the history of the Chosen People. The name *Joshua* means "savior." "Jesus" is a variation of the same name.

The biblical authors, writing probably during the seventh century B.C. (King Josiah's reign), paint a picture of Joshua as an ideal leader, a Moses without flaw. Like Moses, Joshua used spies to judge the strength of the enemy. He also prepared to cross a body of water by celebrating a Passover meal. In addition, he had divine visions, extended his hands to assure victory in battle, and delivered an important farewell address.

The many parallels to Moses suggest that Joshua is a masterful literary creation, an epic of heroic proportions. It is not history in the modern sense of the word. For example, archaeology does not support the massive destruction of Jericho's walls at the time of the invasion of the Promised

Land. The book is religious history. Its primary intent is not to record events as they happened many centuries before but to make theological statements about God's continuing fidelity to the covenant.

The biblical authors wanted to show how Yahweh fulfilled the promises made to Abraham. The Israelites must then fulfill their part of the covenant. They should keep the Law by worshiping the one true God.

The book opens with Joshua preparing for the invasion of Canaan. Joshua could not fail because the Lord guided him: " As long as you live, no one will be able to resist you; I shall be with you as I was with Moses; I shall not fail you or desert you " (Jos 1:5).

To be successful, Joshua must keep close to the Law. But good preparations also helped him. For example, he mustered the support of the Transjordan Israelite tribes, and he set his sights on Jericho as the first city to conquer.

He sent two spies to Jericho to assess the strength of its inhabitants. While they were there, the prostitute Rahab hid them from the king's men. She helped them escape, and in return they instructed her to hang a scarlet cord in the window through which they fled. The Israelites would spare her and her family in the coming slaughter. Rahab's act of kindness to God's people spared her family and earned her a place in history.

Heartened by the news that the Canaanites feared the Israelites, Joshua prepared to enter the Promised Land. When the Lord commanded, the priests led the way across the Jordan River, high from spring flooding, holding up the Ark of the Covenant. When the priests' feet touched the river, the water stopped flowing. Was there a miracle? Did an earthquake temporarily dam the flow so the Israelites could cross? Centuries of storytelling obscure what really happened. What mattered to the Israelites was that God, symbolized by the Ark, led them into the Promised Land, an event celebrated by the erection of a stone altar.

The final preparations for conquest included the circumcision of the new generation of Israelites born in the wilderness, the celebration of a Passover, and Joshua's meeting an angelic host of the Lord's army. In all cases, Joshua obeyed the Lord's commands, a key to later success. When the Israelites obeyed God, they were victorious. When they ignored God and followed their own will, they failed.

■ *discuss* ■

Read Mt 1:1–16. What connection does Rahab have to Jesus?
Read Jas 2:24–25. Why is she praised?

Many scholars believe that Jericho is the world's oldest city. History can never say for sure how the Israelites captured it. The book of Joshua tells a memorable story about crumbling walls. Again, Joshua obeyed what God commanded:

> "All your warriors must march round the city.... Seven priests must carry seven ram's-horn trumpets in front of the ark. On the seventh day ... when the ram's horn sounds ... the entire people must utter a mighty war cry and the city wall will collapse then and there" (Jos 6:3–5).

Did an earthquake happen? Were the walls in disrepair, with only a small population living on the ruins of an earlier city, as archaeology suggests? Did the Israelites tunnel under the city? The biblical authors simply stress that Yahweh was responsible for Israel's success.

Next, the Israelites approached Ai thinking that it would be easy prey. But they were defeated because Aachan had disobeyed God's command to destroy all the booty during the battle of Jericho. Aachan's greed brought a setback for all the people. Only after his death by stoning could the Israelites win the battle. Israel learned an important lesson: disobedience of God leads to death and defeat.

Here we meet a practice that is loathsome by modern standards: the complete destruction of a people and their goods during a holy war. This was part of a practice known as the *ban* (*herem* in Hebrew). Its purpose was to prove that God's people put all their trust in the Lord. He was their leader; they wanted nothing for themselves. From our modern viewpoint, this practice is immoral. But to the ancient people, who only gradually came to understand God's true nature, it exemplified their devotion to God.

Just War

Check a Catholic encyclopedia, a book on morality, or the American bishops' pastoral letter *Challenge of Peace*. Today, Christian teaching limits the violence that can be committed in a war through its principles of a just war.

. journal .

List the conditions for a "just war."

. discuss .

Would you participate in a just war? Why or why not?

■

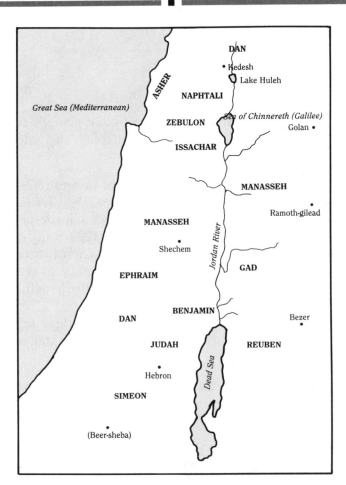

The book ends with two farewell speeches of Joshua (chapters 23–24). The first is an appeal to the people to be faithful to the covenant. The second gives instructions to the twelve tribes to assemble at Shechem to renew the covenant. This was where God promised Abraham that his descendants would receive the Promised Land. The people promised that they would worship only the one true God, and put away false gods. After renewing the covenant and erecting a stone as a witness to the Lord's promises, Joshua dismissed the tribes to their own territories. Joshua died shortly afterward and the people were without a leader.

▪ *discuss* ▪

Israel often erected altars to depict its commitment to God. You may have symbols that show your commitment to the Lord, for example:

- crucifix or religious medal
- your Bible
- daily prayer
- holy picture (icon)

List the religious symbols that show your school's commitment to God. Should your school display any additional symbols? Explain.

Judges.   The main part of the book of Judges (3:7—16:31) collects stories about various "judges" — local, tribal leaders. These charismatic leaders filled a leadership gap between the time of Joshua's death (c. 1200 B.C.) and the beginning of the monarchy (c. 1030 B.C.). Their function was threefold: to defend Israel against its enemies, to settle disputes within and among tribes, and to call the Israelites back to God.

The history of the Israelites under the judges takes the form of a "cycle of apostasy" that follows five stages:

- The Israelites sin by worshiping false gods.
- God punishes them by handing them over to their enemies.
- The Israelites cry out to God to save them from their plight.
- Yahweh takes pity on his people and appoints judges who save them in their distress.
- Once a given judge dies, the cycle repeats itself.

The Israelites' major sin was abandoning the worship of the one Lord for the gods of the Canaanites. The major gods of the Canaanites were the Baals and their female partners, the Astartes. Canaanites believed that the Baals controlled the land. The fertility of the land depended on the Baals

---

Outline of Judges

1. Conquest retold (1:1—3:6)
2. Stories of the Judges (3:7—16:31)
3. History of the tribe of Dan and its idolatry (17:1—18:31)
4. Tribe of Benjamin and its evil (19:1—21:25)

▪ *reading* ▪

Read Judges 2, 6—8, 13—16. Answer the questions in your journal.

1. Briefly summarize the behavior of the Israelites after Joshua's death and God's response to it.
2. How did Gideon respond to God's call? (6:11–24)
3. What ultimately ruined Gideon? (Ch. 8)
4. What do you find most appealing about Samson? What was his greatest character flaw?

having sexual relations with their consorts. The Canaanites believed that they should share in rituals of fertility, including ritual prostitution and drunken orgies, to help bring the divine pair together. They believed that by imitating the action of the gods, they could release the powers that controlled the fertility of land and flocks.

The invading Israelites became farmers as well as keeping their traditional role of shepherds. They turned to the Baals of their new neighbors to insure abundant crops and livestock for themselves. Most likely, the Israelites did not intend to abandon Yahweh; rather they worshiped Yahweh alongside these others gods.

But the Canaanite and Israelite religions were irreconcilable. In essence, Canaanite religion resorted to magic to control the divine beings through properly prescribed rituals. Israel, however, had only one God, and Yahweh condemned the worship of all other gods. Also, while Yahweh bound himself in covenant to the Israelites, revealing himself to be faithful, merciful, and the Lord of all creation, he is clearly beyond human manipulation. Yahweh imposed a strict moral code on his people, which outlawed many of the activities of their Canaanite neighbors.

The task of the judges was to remind the Israelites that they would be punished if they abandoned exclusive worship of the one true God. The judges believed that the Israelites had to defeat the Canaanites in battle to eliminate the temptation to worship false gods.

One of the most widely remembered judges of this time was a woman, Deborah, a prophetess who instructed the general Barak to lead the army. She successfully called a holy war in which the Israelites were victorious. Judges 5 repeats Deborah's story in a poem, one of the oldest pieces in the Bible.

After the Israelites once again abandoned Yahweh, they were attacked by the Midianites to punish them. However, Yahweh raised up a new judge, Gideon (6:1—8:35), despite the young man's objections that he was weak and unworthy. An angel of the Lord assured Gideon that he would lead the Israelites to victory. God gave him the sign of the fleece (6:36–40) to show that Yahweh would deliver Israel through him.

After a number of victories, the people wanted to make Gideon a king. Even though he refused, he asked the people

▪ journal ▪

Gideon claimed he was too weak and unworthy to lead Israel. Describe a time when you thought you were unable to do something asked of you but you came through it "with flying colors."

for gold out of which he fashioned an *ephod*, perhaps a golden idol. Though chosen by God to lead the people, even a judge could do wrong. For his promoting idolatry, Yahweh would eventually punish Gideon's family.

Samson (13:1—16:31) is the most famous judge of all, although scholars are not sure if Samson was the creation of folklore or a real historical person.

The Lord enabled his barren mother to conceive him. In thanksgiving, she vowed he would live as a Nazirite (Nm 6:2–8), one specially dedicated to God. He was to abstain from wine, avoid touching dead bodies, and not cut his hair or beard. The legend surrounding Samson was that his source of strength lay in his long hair. His downfall would come as a result of allowing a woman named Delilah to entice him into revealing this secret. When she cut his hair, he was defeated by his enemies.

The real source of Samson's strength was the spirit of God which enabled him to fight Israel's enemy, the Philistines. Judges 14—16 describes some of his exploits and feats of prodigious strength. He tore apart a lion with his bare hands, destroyed Philistine fields by rigging up torches on the tails of three hundred foxes, killed a thousand Philistines with the jawbone of an ass, and toppled a Philistine temple dedicated to their god Dagon.

Samson's adventures are exciting reading, but they also reveal a man flawed by personal failings who suffered for his infidelities in much the same way Israel suffered throughout its history. When he abandoned the way of the Lord, he abandoned the source of his strength.

The final chapters of Judges show how the nation disintegrated in the absence of strong leaders. Israel was near anarchy, without law: "In those days there was no king in Israel, and everyone did as he saw fit" (Jgs 21:25). It was time for Israel to look to a new form of leadership.

Ruth

The Book of Ruth tells a warm and timeless tale of fidelity and loyalty. Scholars are not sure when it was written or how historical it is. One view holds that it was written after the Exile to offset an official policy that barred intermarriage with foreign women. Ruth is a foreign woman, yet faithful and holy. Yahweh blessed her by making her an ancestor of

David, the greatest Jewish king. Other scholars maintain, however, that Ruth may have been written during Solomon's reign. The book appears between Judges and 1–2 Samuel because its action takes place during the era of the Judges. It ends with a family tree of David, thus pointing to the action of 1–2 Samuel.

The story begins in Moab, a land hostile to Israel. Naomi, her husband, and two sons had gone there to escape famine. Before long, Naomi's husband died. The two sons married Moabite girls. After ten years, the sons also died, leaving Naomi and her two daughters-in-law — Ruth and Orpah — on the brink of poverty.

Eventually, Israel's famine ended and Naomi decided to return to Israel. She instructed Ruth and Orpah to stay with their people and remarry, but Ruth insisted on staying with her mother-in-law:

> "Wherever you go, I shall go,
> wherever you live, I shall live.
> Your people will be my people,
> and your God will be my God" (Ruth 1:16).

The loving Ruth accompanied Naomi to Bethlehem, in Judah, and they arrived there during the barley harvest. Ruth joined the other poor people gleaning the fields for leftover grain after the harvesters passed. There the rich landowner Boaz, a distant relative of Naomi's husband, noticed the Moabite girl. Her story of love and devotion moved him. Naomi, on learning of the meeting, boldly planned to have Boaz marry Ruth.

The Lord blessed Boaz and Ruth with a son, Obed. Obed fathered Jesse who in turn fathered David. Thus, Ruth became the great-grandmother of David and ancestor of Jesus.

Lessons of Ruth.   The story of Ruth teaches God's loving concern for those who suffer in the midst of tragedy. It shows that good comes from family devotion and faithfulness. It also reveals how God's plan of salvation takes place in unexpected ways. Finally, Ruth symbolizes God's utter faithfulness and care for the Chosen People. Her fidelity and devotion mirror God's covenant-love (*hesed*) for his people.

1 and 2 Samuel

The first and second books of Samuel contain stories about some of the most prominent people in the Hebrew

■ *journal* ■

Read the Book of Ruth. Then answer the following questions.

1. List three qualities that describe Ruth's character. Cite the verses that support your descriptions.
2. Write of a time when a friend was loyal to you. What did you feel like at the time?

scriptures, among them Samuel, Saul, and David. The authors drew on many oral traditions and written materials to report this sacred history. They begin with the years of the last judge, Samuel, who anointed Saul the first king of Israel around 1030 B.C. They take the story to around 970 B.C., the end of David's reign.

Written sometime around the time of the Exile, 1–2 Samuel use the literary form of a saga. These books also include some of civilization's earliest historical writing (for example, the summary of David's wars in 2 Sm 8).

Although these books are among the historical books, history is reported from a theological perspective. The writers saw the Lord's hand in choosing David as king and in making Jerusalem the religious capital of the nation. We can find the following themes in these two books:

- God remained with the Israelites when they most needed divine help. The Philistines especially posed a serious threat. Israel needed strong leaders, and a monarchy was set up.

- Israel's leaders, including David, reflected Israel's pattern of infidelity in their own lives. While both the leaders and the nation deserved punishment, God remained with the Chosen People.

- God's mercy preserved Israel from its enemies. This message would inspire the generation of the Babylonian Exile to believe that God would continue to rescue his people. David was the symbol of God's love and concern for the Chosen People. A suffering Israel would look to a new David — the Messiah — to rescue it from new enemies. Christians, of course, believe that Jesus fulfills this promise of a Messiah.

Samuel (read 1 Sm 1—4). Samuel is a transitional figure between the era of the judges and the monarchy. He anointed Israel's first two kings, Saul and David. 1–2 Samuel bear his name because the ancient rabbis thought he authored the books. He displayed great leadership ability as Israel's best judge, but he is most remembered for his role as prophet. He spoke for God in condemning the sons of Eli, preaching repentance, warning of the dangers of kingship, and passing judgment on Saul when he ignored the Lord's commands.

Like other Old Testament figures, the story of Samuel's birth tells us that he was a special gift from God. When the barren Hannah gave birth to Samuel, her beautiful hymn of thanksgiving acknowledged how God helps the weak, confounds the mighty, and lifts up the lowly. In the New Testament, Mary's Magnificat echoes Hannah's prayer as she praises God for making her the mother of the Savior (see Lk 1:46–55).

At the shrine of Shiloh, the priest Eli raised Samuel as God's special servant. God smiled on Samuel while he was serving Eli and called Samuel to the triple vocation of *prophet*, *priest*, and *judge*.

Because of the unjust practices of many of the judges, the people clamored for a king who would rule them "like the other nations" (1 Sm 8:5). This request was an affront to Yahweh who was the sole ruler of Israel. Wanting to be like other nations was clearly the wrong motive for requesting a king; Israel was special, uniquely God's own people.

■ *journal* ■

When God spoke to Samuel, the young boy replied, "Speak, Yahweh; for your servant is listening" (1 Sm 3:10). Think of the different ways God "speaks" to you:

- through your friends
- in the sounds, sights, and smells of nature
- at Mass
- when someone forgives you
- in the love of your parents
- when you pray
- through Bible reading
- when a person in authority justly corrects you

Write of a time when you believe God delivered a message to you. You might share what you wrote with a friend.

Saul (read 1 Sm 9—10).   Samuel warned that a king would draft Israelite children into his army and court, tax the people, and treat them like slaves. Despite these warnings, the Israelites begged Samuel to anoint a king. With God's approval, he eventually singled out Saul to lead God's nation.

Samuel called the tribes together to choose the king by lot. The choice fell on Saul's shoulders, which was interpreted as a sign of divine providence. Samuel warned the people to obey God or he would deal severely with them and their

■ *discuss* ■

What do Sarah, Rebekah, Rachel, Samson's mother, and Hannah have in common?

What is the spiritual message of the birth of their sons?

king. Yahweh gave the people a king, as they wished, but Samuel worried that a king might lead the people away from God.

A key reason Saul became king was his military ability. Before long, however, Saul was filled with pride. He offered sacrifice to God before a battle, a privilege and duty reserved to priests alone. Second, in disobedience to Yahweh, Saul did not kill the king of Amalek or put his town under the *ban* (total destruction) as instructed by Samuel. Saul's sins would exact a price: The Lord would bestow the kingship on another.

David's Youth (read 1 Sm 16:1—19:24). The rest of 1 Samuel tells of Samuel anointing David, the love-hate relationship between Saul and David, Saul's plots to kill David, David's exploits as a vassal of a Philistine king, and Saul's death. The story opens with Yahweh leading Samuel to the youngest son of Jesse, a shepherd boy named David. Samuel anointed him "and the spirit of Yahweh seized on David from that day onwards" (1 Sm 16:13).

In contrast, the spirit of God abandoned Saul, who began to suffer psychological torments such as severe mood shifts. Because of David's reputation as a skilled harpist, he was brought in to soothe Saul's frayed spirits. David's melodic hymns helped Saul. To show his appreciation, Saul made David his armor-bearer.

David was a brave young man. We read the story of his slaying a powerful Philistine warrior named Goliath. Although he was armed only with a slingshot, he relied on God for his strength and defeated Goliath. This tale foreshadows his future career as a military genius and political strategist. Primarily, though, it demonstrates his strong faith in God, the most important quality for a future king of Israel.

At first, Saul loved David. But before long, jealous over David's many gifts, military conquests, and instant popularity, he plotted David's death. 1 Samuel 19—31 tells of Saul's many stratagems to get rid of David. They all failed, however, due in no small measure to Saul's son, Jonathan. Jonathan befriended David and remained loyal to him to death, even renouncing his own claim to the throne. Repeatedly, Jonathan intervened on David's behalf.

Saul's jealous, revengeful attitude turned David into an outlaw. He repeatedly fled Saul, but also gained military victories of his own on behalf of the Israelites. Though persecuted, David's reputation grew. On two occasions, he had the opportunity to kill Saul, but refused to do so because of his own respect for God's anointed one.

Eventually, David became a vassal to the Philistines, although he refused to attack his own people, the Israelites. He used the protection of the Philistines to strengthen his position, awaiting the day when Saul would stop pursuing him so he could serve the people openly.

Meanwhile, the Philistines continued to besiege Saul. He resorted to *necromancy* (summoning the dead) to predict his future. He consulted the witch of Endor and conjured up the ghost of the dead Samuel. Samuel told Saul what he already knew: He must die so David could become king. The Philistines pursued Saul, killed his sons, and wounded the tragic king. Despairing, Saul fell on his sword.

David the King (read 2 Sm 5:1—7:29).   After Saul's death, David became king of Judah in the south, but the northern territory was in the hands of Saul's son Ishbaal. Eventually, Ishbaal quarrelled with his general, Abner, who came over to David's side. David's general Joab killed Abner and two assassins betrayed and killed Ishbaal, all without David's permission. The northern tribes of Israel could now accept David as king. David's rule was to last forty years, seven as ruler over Judah and thirty-three over all of Israel.

David took refuge from Saul at Ein Gedi, near the Dead Sea

David was thirty years old when he united all the tribes into a single nation. This union, which lasted until the end of Solomon's reign, was a golden age. Later generations of Jews would look back on this period as the time when Yahweh especially smiled on his people.

David conquered Jerusalem, at that time a Jebusite city, and made it Israel's capital. Because it hadn't been held by any one of the twelve tribes, it was an ideal site for the center of a unified kingdom. David joyfully brought the Ark of the Covenant to Jerusalem to indicate Yahweh's abiding presence in the midst of the new nation.

David wanted to build a beautiful Temple for the Ark. But the prophet Nathan, speaking for God, revealed instead that Yahweh promised to David a royal dynasty, a promise that led to the belief of a *Messiah* (God's "anointed one"), who would save the Chosen People from their enemies. Christians believe that Jesus is the Christ, the son of David, who came to save not only the Jews but all humanity.

David humbly thanked God for his mercy to the Chosen People: "You are great, Lord Yahweh; there is no one like

Excavations of the Jebusite wall in Jerusalem, dating from David's time

you, no God but you alone, as everything that we have heard confirms. Is there another people on earth like your people, like Israel?" (2 Sm 7:22–23).

David subdued Israel's enemies and built Israel into a powerful nation for the first (and last) time in its history. Good internal organization, an experienced army led by an excellent general, and the decline of other powers such as Egypt to the south and Babylon to the north contributed to the achievements of David's kingship.

The Sinful David (read 2 Sm 11:1—12:15). For all his achievements, David had serious personal faults. His greatest sins were adultery and murder. While one of his soldiers, Uriah, was away, David had sexual relations with Uriah's wife, Bathsheba. She conceived a child. To cover his sin, David brought Uriah back from the war, hoping Uriah would have relations with his wife so he would think the child was his. Uriah, however, refused to sleep with his wife while the Ark of the Covenant was on the battle front, where he felt he should be as well.

David sent Uriah back to the war and instructed his general to put Uriah on the front lines hoping he would be killed in combat. Uriah did, indeed, die in battle. After the proper time for mourning, David married Bathsheba who gave birth to a son who died soon afterwards. Another son born to them, Solomon, would eventually succeed David as king.

Outraged by David's sins, the prophet Nathan told him a parable in which a rich man committed a selfish crime against a poor man. David judged the man in the story worthy of death. Nathan told David, "You are the man!" The shock of the truth brought David to his senses. He grieved deeply over his sins and begged for God's forgiveness.

God did forgive David, but sin has its effect. Nathan tells David that his sins deserved punishment: "Yahweh says this, 'Out of your own household I shall raise misfortune for you'" (2 Sm 12:11). How true this prophecy proved to be! His son Amnon raped a half-sister, Tamar. In revenge, Tamar's brother, Absalom, slew Amnon. David was greatly saddened by this killing, but he decided to spare Absalom's life.

Absalom, however, plotted against his father, undermining the people's love for David. Eventually, he led a rebellion against David, and had himself declared king. David fled Jerusalem, but mustered the support of various allies. Throughout his ordeal, he accepted God's will and continued to love his rebellious son. Eventually, Absalom's forces met those of his father. The rebel forces lost and, against the king's wishes, David's general Joab killed Absalom.

Absalom's death devastated his father. David mourned the death of his beloved son: "... as he wept, he kept saying, 'Oh, my son Absalom! My son! My son Absalom! If only I had died instead of you! Oh, Absalom, my son, my son!'" (2 Sm 19:1).

David gradually won back the tribes that deserted him, and even forgave Saul's family, who had joined in the plot against him. Once again he took the throne and Israel came to order. But David's popularity was not what it once was. Rivalries among the tribes were increasing, and David's judgments were clouded by his favoritism.

David is remembered as Israel's greatest king. He unified the tribes and established Jerusalem as the capital. The Lord made a covenant with him that enabled his dynasty to last for four hundred years, until the Babylonian Captivity in 587 B.C. Yahweh blessed him and, despite his many sins, David remained loyal to his God. Later generations saw in David someone God used to establish the nation as part of the divine plan. In praising David, the Israelites acknowledged the God who continued to favor the Chosen People.

■ *discuss* ■

What do you most admire about David? What do you find least admirable? Why?

■ *focus questions* ■

1. Discuss at least one friendship described in the Hebrew scriptures.
2. Describe the differences in how the books of Joshua and Judges report the conquering of the Promised Land.
3. What was the major function of Israel's judges?
4. What is the meaning of the name *Joshua*? How did he prefigure Christ?
5. In what sense are the books of Joshua, Judges, Ruth, and 1–2 Samuel *historical*?
6. Identify *Rahab*. How did she figure in Israelite history?
7. What is the key message of the book of Joshua?
8. Identify the *ban*. What function did it serve in Israelite history?
9. What cycle of sin repeats itself in the book of Judges?
10. What was the major temptation for Israel toward the Canaanite gods? Contrast Yahweh to these false gods.

11. Discuss the contributions of any two judges.

12. Identify the Philistines. What advantage did they have militarily?

13. Identify Samson.

14. What are the major elements in the story of Ruth? What does this story tell us about God and his relationship with the Israelites?

15. What role did Samuel play in the history of the Chosen People?

16. Why was the kingship eventually taken from Saul and his family?

17. Describe David's youth. What were his most endearing qualities?

18. What were David's major contributions as king?

19. What were David's major sins? How did they return to haunt him?

20. Identify and discuss the significance of the following:

Abner	Eli	Naomi
Bathsheba	Gideon	Nathan
Boaz	Joab	Uriah
Deborah	Jonathan	

▪ exercises ▪

1. List five qualities of a good leader. Write a short essay to explain how either Saul or David measures up to your list.

2. Describe an ideal relationship between a father and a son or a mother and a daughter. Share what you wrote. Did David or Saul exhibit any of your traits in their relationships with their sons Absalom or Jonathan?

3. Compose your own modern version of the book of Ruth.

▪ vocabulary ▪

Copy the meaning of these words into the vocabulary section of your journal.

anarchy
prodigious
transitional

Prayer Reflection

Psalm 51 is a penitential psalm, a lament that begs for God's mercy. The historical setting relates the psalm to David's adultery with Bathsheba, a sin that brought tragedy to David. All of us are sinners and need God's mercy. The words of this psalm can become our words, too.

Have mercy on me, O God, in your faithful love,
in your great tenderness wipe away my offenses;
wash me thoroughly from my guilt,
purify me from my sin.

For I am well aware of my offenses,
my sin is constantly in mind.
Against you, you alone, I have sinned,
I have done what you see to be wrong.

God, create in me a clean heart,
renew within me a resolute spirit.

Give me back the joy of your salvation,
sustain in me a generous spirit.

— Psalm 51:1–4, 10, 12

▪ *reflection* ▪

Review the past week. Examine your relationships with God and others. Identify one thing you are doing (or not doing) that keeps you from being a more loving person.

▪ *resolution* ▪

Ask for God's forgiveness. You might want to celebrate the sacrament of reconciliation. Do something to make up for the harm your sin has caused (for example, help a person you have hurt).

chapter 6

A Kingdom Divided and a Prophetic Word

Israel, come back to Yahweh your God
your guilt was the cause of your downfall.
Say to him, "Take all guilt away
and give us what is good."

— Hosea 14:2, 3

In This Chapter

We will consider:

- Solomon and the divided monarchy
- introduction to the prophets
- ninth-century prophets of the north
- eighth-century prophets of the north

What do you think of the following? The police arrested a man for stealing a loaf of bread. When he appeared before the court, the judge discovered that the man had a family and was without work. He tried as best and honestly as he could to support them. Finally, in desperation, he stole the bread to feed his family. Although the judge sympathized with the man's plight, she was sworn to uphold the law. "I'm sorry, but the law clearly says you must be punished. You stole, and therefore I must punish you. I fine you $100."

But the judge continued, "However, I will give you the money for the fine myself." She reached into her purse and pulled out two fifty-dollar bills and handed them to the defendant.

The judge had more surprises in store. "And I am going to forgive the fine. You may keep the money. Moreover, I am instructing the bailiff to collect five dollars from everyone in this courtroom for being citizens in a city that forces a father to steal to feed his family."

This story exemplifies the justice God bestowed on the Chosen People. The prophets of Israel proclaimed that God loves justice. The essence of divine justice is compassion for the poor, orphans, widows, and those whom society neglects. The judge in the story symbolizes a just God who favorably judges the helpless and firmly corrects the rich and powerful who ignore justice.

The voices of Israel's prophets ring down through the centuries. They teach us that God judges harshly those who fail to live the covenant. But Yahweh's justice is also merciful and gracious, flowing like a mighty mountain stream to wipe away the conditions of oppression.

In this chapter, we will introduce some of the major prophets whose powerful words called unfaithful kings to honor the covenant. Infidelity to God and injustice to the

113

people led to the division of the kingdom. We will see how this sad state of affairs eventually led to the obliteration of the northern kingdom by Assyria in 721 B.C.

■

Commitment to Justice

Justice was a key theme in the ministry of the prophet Amos. Listen to his thundering voice: "Let justice flow like water, and uprightness like a never-failing stream" (Am 5:24).

Today, many justice issues demand the attention of Christians and all people of good will. Check off five of the following pressing issues that you believe demand our greatest concern. Then rank these five from **1** (most important) to **5** (least important).

_____ sexual exploitation
_____ abortion
_____ women's rights
_____ education of minorities
_____ war
_____ hunger
_____ crime
_____ terrorism

_____ pollution of the environment
_____ unemployment
_____ underdevelopment of Third World nations
_____ disparity of wealth
_____ violence in the media
_____ poverty

■ *discuss* ■

Review the newspapers and list five other important justice issues.

■ *evaluate* ■

The prophet Isaiah warns: "Learn to do good, search for justice, discipline the violent, be just to the orphan, plead for the widow" (Is 1:17). Justice is everyone's concern. What do you think about the following statements?

1. The poor we will always have with us. What's the use of trying to overcome such a massive problem as poverty?

    ☐ Agree   ☐ Disagree   ☐ Not sure

2. The church should lead the way in solving social justice issues.

    ☐ Agree   ☐ Disagree   ☐ Not sure

3. I can make a difference. As the Christopher Movement
   puts it: "It is better to light one candle than to curse the
   darkness."

   ☐ Agree   ☐ Disagree   ☐ Not sure

▪ *journal* ▪

Select one of the issues in this exercise and read two recent
articles on it. Include at least one article from a Catholic
magazine, journal, or newspaper. Prepare a short report on
the following:

a. the scope of the problem
b. church teaching
c. something a teen can do to help

1 and 2 Kings

Deuteronomist editors compiled these two books, beginning in King Josiah's reign and finishing their work sometime during the Babylonian Captivity. These books span the
era of Israelite history from the death of David around 970
B.C. through the split of the northern and southern kingdoms in 922 B.C., to the destruction of the northern kingdom
by Assyria in 721 B.C. and through the Babylonian Captivity
of the southern kingdom in 587/6 B.C.

Two theological themes predominate. To turn from true
worship of God and to neglect and abuse the poor and
helpless invite God's judgment. The destruction of the northern kingdom and the captivity of the southern kingdom
resulted from a defiant turning away from God and a disre-
gard for God's commandments.

The second theme, as we have seen before, is that God still
cared for the Chosen People and repeatedly sent prophets to
warn of the ruination caused by sin.

Solomon

The first eleven chapters of 1 Kings tell of the reign of
Solomon, son of David and Bathsheba. Before David's death,
his oldest son Adonijah thought he would certainly inherit
David's throne. The prophet Nathan, however, had Solomon

Outline of 1 and 2 Kings

1. David's death (1 Kgs 1:1—1 Kgs 2:11)
2. Solomon's reign (1 Kgs 2:12—1 Kgs 11:43)
3. History of the divided kingdom (1 Kgs 12—2 Kgs 17)
4. Judah's history until its fall (2 Kgs 18:1—2 Kgs 25:30)

▪ *reading* ▪

Read 1 Kgs 3, 6, 8. Answer the questions in your journal.

1. What is Solomon's request? How does God reply?
2. How does Solomon prove his wisdom in 3:16–28?
3. How was the Temple decorated? What were some of the objects placed in the Temple?
4. List three petitions Solomon prays for in this prayer of dedication.

anointed king by the priest Zadok before Adonijah assumed power. Deserted by his supporters, Adonijah fled for his life, taking sanctuary at the altar.

Before David died, he counseled Solomon to keep the Mosaic Law to guarantee a prosperous reign. He also instructed Solomon to rid the kingdom of all threats to the monarchy. As soon as David died, Solomon did indeed rid himself of his rivals: his brother Adonijah; Joab, David's cunning general; and the rebel Shimei. He also banished the influential priest Abiathar and, in his place, appointed Zadok.

Before long, Solomon established himself as a powerful king with few rivals in the ancient Mediterranean world. His kingdom flourished as he cemented relations with foreign powers and organized the kingdom along Egyptian methods of administration. He also expanded trade, modernized his army, built fortifications throughout his kingdom, and established a glorious court that was the envy of other monarchs.

Solomon has a well-deserved reputation as a great builder. His reign was peaceful and very prosperous. Politically, he established a complex series of treaties, marriages, and diplomacy. Among his countless wives and concubines was pharaoh's daughter. A visit by the famed Queen of Sheba (1 Kings 10) illustrated the renown of Solomon's achievements as she stood in awe of his wealth and wisdom.

Solomon's most magnificent achievement was building the Temple that became the center of Israel's religious life. 1 Kings 6—7 describes Solomon's Temple and palace complex. And 1 Kings 8 recalls Solomon's Temple dedication speech. Solomon asked God to receive the prayers and sacrifices of the people who would worship in the Temple. He also warned the people to obey the commandments of God's covenant.

1 Kings 9 tells of Solomon's vision, which indicated that God accepted the Temple dedicated to him. Once again, Yahweh renewed the promises made to David's family, but also warned that if Solomon or any of his descendants worshiped false gods, he would destroy the Temple dedicated in his name.

The expression "the wisdom of Solomon" has biblical roots. At the start of his reign, Solomon prayed for an understanding heart to judge the people and a spirit to discern right from wrong. God granted Solomon his request, and scripture tells us that "God gave Solomon immense wisdom and understanding, and a heart as vast as the sand on the seashore" (1 Kgs 5:9).

Though Solomon was wise, he was also a fool. Power and the splendor of his office corrupted him and turned him from God. Economically, he overextended his resources. For example, a symbol of a king's wealth was to keep a large harem. Solomon's harem was immense, numbering "seven hundred wives of royal rank and three hundred concubines" (1 Kgs 11:3). Because of their royal background, Solomon had to support them in luxury and provide them with servants.

Further, he had to build roads and garrisons for his large army and provide the soldiers with horses and chariots. Solomon's many building campaigns also strained the nation. He maintained a vigorous trade with other nations and levied tariffs on goods transported through Israel. Nevertheless, he also taxed his fellow Israelites to the breaking point. Eventually he forced 30,000 of his own people to work as serfs one month out of every three. The people began to grumble and even to talk of rebellion.

Many of the foreign princesses Solomon brought into his harem introduced their gods and priests into the land. Many Israelites, Solomon included, began to worship these false gods in addition to Yahweh. All of this led to Solomon's punishment.

> Yahweh was angry with Solomon because his heart had turned away from Yahweh, God of Israel.... Yahweh therefore said to Solomon, "Since you have behaved like this and have not kept my covenant or the laws which I laid down for you, I shall tear the kingdom away from you and give it to one of your servants. For your father David's sake, however, I shall not do this during your lifetime, but shall tear it out of your son's hands. Even so, ... for the sake of my servant David, ...I shall leave your son one tribe" (1 Kgs 11:9, 11–13).

Yahweh's word was truth. Rebellions from within and without began to plague Solomon's kingdom. The prophet Ahijah promised Solomon's servant Jeroboam that he would eventually rule over the northern tribes. Rehoboam, Solomon's son, would rule in the south, commanding the loyalty of only the tribe of Judah. After Solomon's death in 922 B.C., Jeroboam led a successful revolt against Solomon's heir, which tore the kingdom apart.

▪ *discuss* ▪

How important is it today for the head of the nation to be a man or woman of faith? Explain.

The Divided Monarchy

After the revolt of the northern tribes, there were two kingdoms: in the north, Israel, which included ten tribes of the old alliance; in the south, Judah, made up of descendants of the tribe of Judah and some descendants of Simeon. Though numerically much smaller than Israel, the southern kingdom was more tightly united. It remained devoted to David's family and centered its worship on the Temple in Jerusalem which housed the Ark of the Covenant.

The northern kingdom had richer and more prosperous land. Jeroboam centered worship at two ancient shrines — Dan and Bethel. Later Jews would explain Assyria's destruction of the northern kingdom by pointing to Israel's failure to worship Yahweh in the holy city of Jerusalem. Instead, its kings turned to pagan gods and practices.

1 Kings 12—16 record the early days of the divided monarchy. These chapters alternately treat the reigns of the kings of the north and then of the south. The authors of 1 and 2 Kings, writing from the perspective of the southern kingdom, found little that was good in the reigns of the northern kings. They felt these kings were largely to blame for the tragedy that befell the nation.

A significant northern king was Omri (c. 876–869). He seized the throne, moved the capital to the city of Samaria, and established relations with Phoenicia by marrying his son Ahab to the wily princess Jezebel. Omri also expanded Israel's territory by defeating the king of Moab.

After Omri's death, his weak son Ahab ascended the throne. Tragically, he allowed his wife, Jezebel, to erect altars to the pagan god Baal. The king and the people quickly fell into idolatry. As a result, Yahweh sent prophets to call the Chosen People back to just living and true worship of the only Lord.

Who Were the Prophets?

God sent prophets to the Chosen People at those times in their history when they most needed to hear and remember God's word. Israel and Judah's decline as a strong and unified kingdom and the period of the Babylonian Captivity gave rise to Israel's greatest prophets. Leaders and people alike needed to hear the basic message of the prophets:

"Repent of your foolish ways and God will save you. Fail to repent and you and the nation will be doomed."

Spokesmen for God.   The Hebrew word for prophet was *nabi*, which meant "spokesman" or "mouthpiece." The first and greatest *nabi* was Moses who heard Yahweh's message and then delivered it to the people. The Hebrew scriptures also call Aaron a *nabi* because he served as Moses' spokesman. Samuel, the last of the judges, also had the role of priest and prophet. His inspired leadership foreshadowed the role of future prophets. Though he anointed Saul king, Samuel also felt free to call Saul to fidelity. At the Lord's urging, he warned that obedience to God's law is better than sacrifice. Nathan, too, played this prophetic role in David's court.

The term *nabi* also referred to a group of holy men who engaged in trancelike behavior. Most of them served as part of the king's court. These "court prophets" prophesied more what the king wanted to hear than the true word of the living God. The Hebrew scriptures do not have much respect for these guilds of prophets and contrast their words and behavior to that of the true prophets of God.

Writing Prophets Versus Speaking Prophets.   Some Old Testament prophets are called "writing prophets," while others are known as "speaking prophets." Elijah and Elisha, whose stories 1 and 2 Kings record, are often called "speaking prophets" because they do not have biblical books named after them. They lived about one hundred years before the great era of Hebrew prophecy and spoke God's message to the people of their day.

The so-called "writing prophets" spoke the message God entrusted to them, but they also have books named after them. In some cases (for example, Amos and Micah) their disciples may have repeated and handed on their spoken messages before committing them to writing. In other cases, the prophets themselves wrote their own messages.

Major Prophets Versus Minor Prophets.   Tradition divides the prophetical books into two groups — the major and minor prophets. We might conclude that the so-called major prophets delivered a more important message than the minor prophets. However, this is not the case. The messages of all the prophets are important, and the basic messages have many similarities. *Major* and *minor* refer to the length of the prophetical books. Each of the major prophets took up one scroll while the twelve minor prophets together were all written on the same single scroll. Here is a list of the prophetical books in the Catholic Bible:

Major prophets	Minor prophets	
Isaiah	Amos	Nahum
Jeremiah *	Hosea	Habakkuk
Ezekiel	Micah	Zephaniah
Daniel **	Joel	Haggai
	Jonah	Zechariah
	Obadiah	Malachi

* Two additional short prophetical books — Lamentations and Baruch — traditionally have been associated with Jeremiah.

** Catholic Bibles include Daniel as a prophetic book because of its prophecies about the Day of the Lord. However, the Jews place it among the Writings.

Former Prophets Versus Later Prophets. In the Hebrew canon, the books of Joshua, Judges, 1 and 2 Samuel, and 1 and 2 Kings are called the "Former Prophets." Isaiah, Jeremiah, and Ezekiel, plus the minor prophets are called the "Later Prophets." The early Jewish editors referred to the earlier, "historical" books as prophetical for three reasons: 1) they contain "religious" history that treats Israel's relationship with God and the results of disobedience, the major theme of all the prophetical books; 2) tradition assigned three prophetical figures as the authors of these books: Joshua and Samuel for the books named after them and Jeremiah for 1 and 2 Kings; 3) prophets such as Samuel, Gad, Nathan, Elijah, Elisha, Isaiah, and Jeremiah all play key roles in the story of the historical books (1 and 2 Kings provide much background information to the careers of the prophets who ministered before the Babylonian Exile).

Some Characteristics of the Prophets. In general, we can observe the following about the prophets:

■ *The prophet received an irresistible call from God.* Amos, for example, testified how God took him from his occupation as a shepherd (Am 7:15) and he felt compelled to respond to God's call (Am 3:8).

■ *The divine message seized the prophets in different ways.* Prophets could receive God's word through dreams, visions, by hearing, or by internal inspiration. Ezekiel, for example, had overpowering visions.

■ *The prophets felt compelled to speak God's word, and they did so in many ways.* Often the prophet used the formula, "Thus says the Lord...." Sometimes the prophet would dramatize the message through bizarre, extravagant, and symbolic actions. For example, Jeremiah wore a wooden yoke to symbolize the future slavery of his people. The prophets spoke their messages in many ways: through stories, direct speech, poetry, sermons, proverbs, love songs, satire, diatribes, funeral songs, and the like. Thus, the prophet would use whatever means he could to catch the attention of his audience and deliver God's message.

■ *The prophet usually stood alone and was unpopular with the establishment.* The true prophet's message typically went against the nation and the king who represented the people. Kings believed that by getting rid of the prophet, the message he spoke would not come to pass. We see this clearly in the career of Elijah. Ahab and Jezebel hounded him to the point that he feared for his life.

■ *The prophet's message had both a present and a future dimension.* The prophet's primary vocation was to deliver God's message to the people of his own time. This message was always urgent. At times, the prophet foretold some event that would happen in the near future to prove the divine source of his mission and message. Prophets did not usually concern themselves with the distant future. Even when prophets looked to the final triumph of God, their message about the end of time involved important lessons for their own generation. In general, the message of the prophets predicted punishment for unrepented sins or prosperity for heeding God's warning.

■ *One could not always tell who was a true prophet.* False prophets appear from time to time in the Old Testament. Their external behavior and words were similar to that of the true prophets. People would recognize the true prophets by the prophecy being fulfilled and, more important, by the fact that the prophet's teaching was in line with true doctrine about Yahweh.

Key Themes in Prophetic Teaching. The prophets repeated three main teachings:

1. *There is only one true God — Yahweh.* God loves his people. God is the creator of heaven and earth and the Lord of all nations. All others gods are powerless; in fact, they don't even exist.

2. *The one God is holy and demands that we renounce sin.* God's holiness transcends all creation. God calls a special people to him and commands them to be holy, but sin keeps people from God. It must be rooted out from the lives of individuals and from the life of the nation.

Prophets remind the people that the covenant law shows the path to holiness. In a special way, the covenant demands worshiping God in truth and a passionate commitment to justice.

3. *The Messiah.* The later prophets promised that God would not abandon the divine promises, even though the people deserved punishment. God would save a "remnant" of the people. In a future age, God would shower his blessings on the people. He would set up an ideal kingdom ruled by the "anointed one" (*Messiah* in Hebrew).

This Messiah, the Christ, would be a descendant of David. Later prophets would see this earthly king as a savior, a servant of Yahweh. He would preach the Law in truth and would even sacrifice his own life for the people. Christians, of course, believe all the messianic prophecies converge in Jesus of Nazareth.

Ninth-Century Prophets of the Northern Kingdom

Elijah (read 1 Kings 17—19; 21). Elijah's name symbolizes the major theme of his mission: "My God is Yahweh." Living under the reign of Ahab in the northern kingdom in the ninth century B.C., Elijah did all he could to promote worship of the only true God. Ahab's marriage to the Phoenician princess Jezebel was economically and politically helpful to Israel, but religiously it was a disaster. Jezebel imported to Israel her Baals and prophets of pagan religion. She persuaded Ahab to erect an altar and temple to Baal in Samaria. This outrage spurred Elijah into action. 1 Kings tells us that Elijah called down a famine on the land, hoping this punishment would shock Israel back to fidelity.

Yahweh Is the Only True God. Eventually, Elijah challenged Ahab's pagan prophets to prove that their gods were more powerful than Yahweh. At the top of Mount Carmel, Elijah taunted the ineffective prophets to call on their gods to send down fire to consume a sacrifice. When the prophets of the Baals failed, Yahweh vindicated Elijah by sending fire to consume both the holocaust and the altar. The people were awestruck, fell to their knees, and proclaimed, "Yahweh is God, Yahweh is God!"

Elijah had the false prophets put to death, and, shortly after, heavy rains descended on the land. The famine was over. Yahweh proved that the word of his prophet was true.

When Jezebel heard of Elijah's actions, she plotted his death. Elijah fled for his life. He complained to God about his condition and wanted to die. An angel of the Lord brought him food and water in the desert, telling him to journey to the mountain of God. On Mount Horeb, God spoke to Elijah in a "still small voice." God told Elijah not to despair. Elijah would find the people who had remained faithful, including Elisha, the prophet who succeeded Elijah, and Jehu, who would be anointed as the new king of Israel.

Care for the Poor. 1 Kings 21 reports how Ahab coveted the vineyard of a poor man, Naboth. Naboth refused to surrender his rightful claim to it to the greedy and avaricious king. Jezebel conspired to arrange Naboth's death so her husband could take possession of the vineyard. When Elijah heard of this cruelty, he confronted Ahab and prophesied doom for his family. God would not tolerate cruelty to the poor. Yahweh is a just God, one who protects and cares for the poor and helpless.

Ahab met his death by a chance shot in battle. His son Ahaziah reigned only a short time. Elijah predicted his death for consulting the pagan god Baal-Zebub, the "Baal of Flies." Another son, Jehoram, reigned for eleven years, but he also died from a battle wound. He died childless, so the prophet Elisha anointed Jehu king and it was Jehu who assassinated Jezebel.

Significance of Elijah (read 2 Kgs 2:1–14). Elijah ranks next to Moses as a great prophet of the Old Testament. Often he symbolizes the Prophets in the same way Moses symbolizes the Law. The biblical authors, writing some two hundred years after Elijah, underscored the importance of this extraordinary man by describing a whirlwind in which Yahweh bears Elijah to heaven in a fiery chariot.

Elijah lived in the imaginations of future generations of Jews. He was seen as one who would bring peace to the world at the end of time. He would be the precursor and

■ *journal* ■

Write of a time when you met God in the silence of your own heart.

partner of the Messiah. He would interpret properly the mysteries of the Law. The New Testament records the impact of this great prophet. For example, many people thought that Jesus himself was Elijah. Jesus, however, identified John the Baptist as Elijah. And the gospels of Matthew, Mark, and Luke tell us that Elijah, along with Moses, was present at Jesus' transfiguration.

Elisha, Successor to Elijah (please read 2 Kgs 2, 4—5, 9). Scripture tells us that Elisha inherited Elijah's mantle when Elijah was transported to heaven, symbolizing his taking on Elijah's prophetic vocation and power. Unlike Elijah, who traveled alone, Elisha worked with a group, "the sons of the prophets."

Like Elijah, Elisha was a wonder-worker. He raised the dead to life, multiplied food, cleansed poisoned water, and helped Israel win a war. In addition, he performed many other miraculous deeds. However, he also met abuse from being true to his vocation.

Elisha's death marks the end of the ninth-century prophets. They tried to purge Israel of Baal-worship, but their efforts did not last. Like Elijah, Elisha is known more for his deeds than his spoken words. We will see that the eighth century produced the greatest prophets of the spoken oracle and written word.

Eighth-Century Prophets of the North (Amos and Hosea)

Jehu and his successors ruled for around seventy-five years. Through uneasy treaties, they held off the fierce Assyrians. Finally, Jeroboam II came to power in Israel. His prosperous and peaceful reign lasted forty years (786–746 B.C.). It looked as though Israel had entered another golden age.

But Jeroboam II and his successors, who lasted until the Assyrian destruction of the northern kingdom in 721 B.C., were religiously corrupt and morally bankrupt. They returned to the worship of the Baals and the scandalous exploitation of the poor by the rich. God sent two important prophets — Amos and Hosea — to warn the people of impending doom.

Amos: Do What Is Right.   Amos was a shepherd and tree farmer from Tekoa, near Bethlehem in the southern kingdom. God's call directed him to preach to the northern kingdom around 750 B.C., during King Jeroboam II's reign.

Amos is the prophet of social justice. His basic message had interlocking components: worship of God must show itself in concrete deeds of mercy and justice to the weak and the poor. Amos fearlessly proclaimed to the northern kingdom its many sins: genocide, cruelty, anger, dishonesty, greed, lawlessness, sexual excess, desecration of the dead, rejection of the prophets, robbery, violence, selfishness, deceit, injustice, and pride.

Amos warned that this behavior would lead to destruction. He prophesied God's impending judgment of the nation. He called the nation to repentance, saying that God really wants people to

> Hate evil, love good,
> let justice reign at the city gate:
> it may be that Yahweh, God Sabaoth,
> will take pity on the remnant of Joseph (Am 5:15).

For Amos, justice was a dynamic reality. Its power is life-giving: "Let justice flow like water, and uprightness like a never-failing stream!" (Am 5:24).

Though Amos did not believe the people would repent in time to avert God's punishment, he still maintained hope. A small "remnant" would survive the impending destruction (3:12). God would sift out the bad and raise up the kingdom of David (9:11).

Predictably, Israel's leaders did not like Amos' message, so they banished him (7:12), but his message remained to challenge Israel to repent before the day of doom would descend on the nation. Amos' message stands today to challenge all nations, especially the rich ones, to passionately serve the poor in their midst.

Outline of Amos

1. Judgment of the nations (1:1—2:16)
2. Prophetic sermons for Israel (3:1—6:14)
3. Symbolic visions of Amos: threats and promises (7:1—8:8)
4. Epilogue: messianic perspective (8:9—9:15)

■ *journal* ■

Please read the following passages from Amos and answer the questions in your journal.

1. Am 1:1 and 7:10–15

Describe Amos and his vocation.

2. Am 4:6–11

What signs from God did Israel ignore?

3. Amos 7—8

Interpret the meaning of Amos' visions: locusts, fire, plumb-line, and basket of ripe fruit.

■ *research* ■

Obtain a copy of the American bishops' document, *Economic Justice for All*.

1. Read the introduction. List the six principal themes of the pastoral letter (No. 13–18).
2. Refer to Chapter 2 of *Economic Justice for All*, entitled "The Christian Vision of the Economic Life." Quickly look over Nos. 28–60. Then focus on Nos. 38–40. Write a brief paragraph describing what justice means from the perspective of the Hebrew scriptures.

Hosea: Love Loyalty.   Hosea was born and prophesied in the northern kingdom. His career overlapped the last years of Amos' ministry, probably spanning the years 745 B.C. to after the fall of Israel. He saw the last years of Jeroboam II's reign and the final years of Israel's monarchy, including the assassination of four kings. His contemporaries were two prophets of the southern kingdom, First Isaiah and Micah (see Chapter 7 below).

We know little of Hosea. He may have been a priest. The book opens with God commanding Hosea to marry a harlot. His wife, Gomer, may have been a temple prostitute. Another opinion is that she may not have originally been a prostitute but later became one. In either case, Hosea remained loyal to Gomer and loved her despite her terrible sin. Hosea always remained willing to forgive her.

Outline of Hosea

1. Hosea's life as prophecy (1—3)
2. Hosea's prophetic judgments on Israel (4—13)
3. Future blessing if Israel repents (14)

Hosea drew on his painful relationship with his wife to describe Yahweh's relationship with Israel. As Gomer abandoned him, so Israel became an unfaithful lover who ignored God's covenant. Hosea, like Amos, saw Israel's worst crimes as idolatry and ruthless oppression of the poor.

Biographical Theology.   Hosea was the first prophet to draw on the rich image of marriage to describe God's compassionate covenant love for Israel. The image also allowed him to describe Israel's infidelity as adultery.

Chapters 1 through 3 of Hosea are biographical. A good example of Hosea's drawing on his own experience involves the symbolic naming of his and Gomer's children to teach the nation important lessons and shock it into repentance. He named the oldest son *Jezreel* to recall Jehu's savage slaying of Ahab's descendants when he assumed power. This name portended the slaughter that would befall an unrepentant Israel at the hands of the Assyrians.

He named their daughter *Lo-ruhama*, which means "she is not pitied." Yahweh declared that he would no longer show compassion for an Israel that had always taken that love and protection for granted. Finally, the third child (a son), was called *Lo-ammi*, meaning "not my people." The name served notice: Yahweh will disown the Chosen People, no longer recognizing Israel as his own.

▪ *journal* ▪

1. Read Hos 1—3. Note the sins of Gomer/Israel. What does chapter 3 say about the outcome of the unfaithful love affair between Hosea/Gomer, Yahweh/Israel?

2. Read Hos 14. Note the result of sincere conversion. Is this a hopeful passage? Explain.

▪ *discuss* ▪

1. If Hosea lived in our society, what major crimes would he warn us against? What evidence is there in today's world that people are not faithful to God?

2. Discuss at least five signs that God's tender love is clearly alive in our world today.

3. Do people need to hear a strong word of correction when they stray from God's laws? Explain your answer.

4. Does the fear of punishment and even hell keep some people on the right path? Explain.

Key Themes in Hosea. The following themes characterize Hosea's message:

▪ *Israel is guilty of sin.* Hosea acknowledged the enormity of Israel's sins. He uses the imagery of a lawsuit to prosecute his case against the northern kingdom:

> Israelites, hear what Yahweh says,
> for Yahweh indicts the citizens of the country:
> there is no loyalty, no faithful love,

> no knowledge of God in the country,
> only perjury and lying, murder, theft,
> adultery and violence,
> bloodshed after bloodshed (Hos 4:1–2).

■ *Israel does not know God.*   Israel's basic problem is that it rejected a true understanding of God. As Gomer did not understand Hosea's deep love for her, Israel did not understand all the good Yahweh had done on its behalf.

> Since you yourself have rejected knowledge,
> so I shall reject you from my priesthood;
> since you have forgotten the teaching of your God,
> I in my turn shall forget your children (Hos 4:6).

Not knowing God leads to false ritualism and the exploitation of the poor. Its antidote is clear:

> For faithful love is what pleases me, not sacrifice;
> knowledge of God, not burnt offerings (Hos 6:6).

■ *Israel's sins deserve punishment.*   Israel's crimes cried out for retribution. The nation's stubborn refusal to return to God demanded divine justice. Hard-heartedness made the nation wicked and perverse:

> You have ploughed wickedness,
> you have reaped iniquity,
> you have eaten the fruit of falsehood.
> Because you have trusted in your chariots,
> in your great numbers of warriors,
> turmoil is going to break out among your people,
> and all your fortresses will be laid waste (Hos 10:13–14).

■ *Despite Israel's sin, God loves it with a wholehearted, steadfast love.*   The Lord has a deep personal relationship with his chosen ones, like a husband to his wife, or a father to his son.

Hosea warned of impending destruction and called the nation to repentance. However, we best remember him for the more important theme of God's undeserved, tender love for his chosen ones. God would never abandon his people:

> Israel, how could I give you up? . . .
> My heart within me is overwhelmed,
> fever grips my inmost being.
> I will not give rein to my fierce anger,

> I will not destroy Ephraim again,
> for I am God, not man,
> the Holy One in your midst,
> and I shall not come to you in anger (Hos 11:8–9).

Hosea's reassuring words of God's love did not save the northern kingdom from its immediate fate. King Tiglath-pileser restored Assyria to its former power. He captured Babylon and began his march toward Egypt. The Israelite kings refused to face the inevitable as they foolishly tried to get Egyptian support. Their efforts backfired and led to Israel's destruction by Tiglath-pileser's son, Shalmaneser V. Sargon II, in turn, succeeded him. He deported over 27,000 Israelites into exile. These exiles were the "Lost Tribes of Israel" who eventually intermarried with the peoples of their new lands, thus losing their identity as God's Chosen People.

The dreaded day prophesied by Hosea had come.

> The days of punishment have come,
> the days of retribution are here;
> Israel knows it! (Hos 9:7).

The fate of the northern kingdom was sealed. In our next chapter, we will study the fate of the southern kingdom, Judah. It, too, saw God's punishment in its fall to Babylon. But the experience of the Exile would cause the nation to repent. And once again, as Hosea confidently prophesied, God's love would tenderly draw the Chosen People to him.

■ *focus questions* ■

1. Discuss one of the major themes of 1–2 Kings.

2. What were some of the high and low points of Solomon's reign?

3. To what do the biblical authors attribute the divided monarchy?

4. What was the role of a *prophet*? Distinguish between prophets such as Elijah and Amos and the "court prophets."

5. What distinguishes the "speaking prophets" from the "writing prophets"?

6. What is the difference between the major and minor prophets? Who are the major prophets?

■ *discuss* ■

"God upsets the comfortable and comforts the upset." Explain how this maxim applies to Hosea.

■ *journal* ■

1. Do people take advantage of someone who is always forgiving? Explain. Do you?

2. Read 2 Kings 17. List some of the reasons the author offers for the destruction of Israel.

7. Discuss three characteristics of the prophets.

8. How could one recognize a true prophet?

9. Discuss the major themes in prophetic teaching.

10. Discuss one of the major themes in the preaching of Elijah. Describe his role in Jewish history. What impact did he have in New Testament times?

11. Discuss a major accomplishment of the prophet Elisha.

12. Discuss the background and one aspect of the message of Amos.

13. What is justice from the viewpoint of Amos or Hosea? What image for justice does Amos use?

14. What key image did Hosea use to describe God's covenant love with the Israelites? How did this image flow from Hosea's own experience?

15. Why did Hosea give bizarre names to his children?

16. Characterize the message of Hosea.

17. What happened to the northern kingdom (Israel) in 721 B.C.?

18. Identify the following:

Rehoboam	Jeroboam II
Jeroboam	Gomer
Ahab	Sargon II
Jezebel	Lost Tribes of Israel
Naboth	

▪ *exercises* ▪

Be a prophet:

a. Review the mini-research assignment you did in the opening exercise, entitled "Commitment to Justice." Recall that you read two recent articles about a social justice topic.

b. Find the address of the "Letters to the Editor" section of your local newspaper or a legislator or member of the executive branch of the government.

c. Write to a person listed in "b" above. Explain a few facts about the social justice issue you have chosen and why the problem concerns you as a young person. Suggest a course of action for the readers of the newspaper or the government official to whom you write.

▪ *vocabulary* ▪

Copy the meaning of the following words into the vocabulary section of your journal:

desecration   retribution   taunt

d. Be sure to sign your letter and include your return address. If you write to a government official, you will probably receive a reply. If you write to a newspaper, your letter may be published. Share and discuss with your classmates any response you get from this project.

Prayer Reflection

Psalm 54 is an appeal to the God of justice. Its message is for all time.

> God, save me by your name,
> in your power vindicate me.
> God, hear my prayer,
> listen to the words I speak.
>
> Arrogant men are attacking me,
> bullies hounding me to death,
> no room in their thoughts for God.
>
> But now God is coming to my help,
> the Lord, among those who sustain me.
>
> — Psalm 54:1–4

▪ *reflection* ▪

Where do you most need help from the Lord in your life right now?

▪ *resolution* ▪

Examine how you treat your classmates, family members, and co-workers. Do you treat people with respect and give them what they deserve? If not, do something this coming week to help right any wrong you might have committed against someone.

chapter 7

The Fall of Judah and Exile

"You have already been told what is right
and what Yahweh wants of you.
Only this, to do what is right,
to love loyalty
and to walk humbly with your God."

— Micah 6:8

In This Chapter

We will look at the following topics:

- Judah from 922 B.C. to 721 B.C. and beyond:

  — First Isaiah and Micah

- Judah up to the Exile

  — Jeremiah

- the minor prophets

- Ezekiel

A man was walking along a narrow path, not looking where he was going. Suddenly, he slipped over the edge of a cliff. As he fell, he grabbed a sturdy branch that grew from the side of the cliff. He soon realized that he could not hang on for long, so he cried for help.

Man: Is there anyone up there? I need help.

Voice: Yes, I'm here!

Man: Who are you?

Voice: The Lord, your God.

Man: Lord, help me!

Voice: Do you trust me?

Man: I trust you completely, Lord.

Voice: Good. Let go of the branch.

Man: What did you say?

Voice: Let go of the branch.

Man: [After a long pause] Is anyone else up there?

This oft-repeated story shows an unwillingness to trust the Lord. This was certainly the case with the southern kingdom of Judah in its last days. Despite repeated warnings from the prophets, it stubbornly clung to two major evils: idolatry and injustice. Eventually, this led to the destruction of Jerusalem and Solomon's Temple and mass deportations of the leading citizens to Babylon.

God Calls

Read the first chapter of Jeremiah, which tells of his vocation. Jeremiah at first protested God's call, but the Lord assured him of divine protection.

All followers of Jesus have a call to continue his work among the people we meet. One of our Christian duties is to be prophets for the Lord, to speak his word in today's world. Though we may feel unworthy of the call, the Lord promises that he will supply what we lack.

Here is a list of traits that would be helpful for being a spokesperson for Christ. Use the following scale to rate how well you exhibit these in your own life. Add three others to the list.

3 — describes me well
2 — describes me somewhat
1 — does not describe me

____ friendly	____ emotionally stable	____ confident
____ ability to handle criticism	____ authentic	____ good judgment
____ truthful	____ hard worker	____ can accept challenges
____ sensitive	____ ability to laugh at self	____ courageous
____ tactful	____ self-motivator	____ _____
____ powerful speaker	____ prayerful	____ _____
____ intelligent		____ _____

▪ journal ▪

How would you react if a favorite priest or sister told you that you would make a good priest, brother, or nun? How should you react? Do you think the Lord *might* be calling you to a religious vocation? Explain.

▪ discuss ▪

1. Which three traits are most important for a person whose vocation is God's work?

2. List and discuss five common situations in which today's teens can speak for the Lord.

Judah From 922–721 B.C. and Beyond: Isaiah and Micah

Judah was a small kingdom that included the hills around Jerusalem and spreading into the Negev desert. Farming, sheep-herding, and trade with Egypt and Arabia were its economic mainstays. Politically, Judah found itself enmeshed in various struggles, alliances, and intrigues involving a series of corrupt kings. Solomon's son, Rehoboam, and grandson were unfaithful. The next two kings — Asa and Jehoshaphat — were reformers who tried to keep alive the covenant. Their successors, however, married into the Ahab-Jezebel family with tragic results. The same evils that befell Israel in the north were infecting the spirit of David's own

country: idolatry, injustice, and empty religious rituals. God
sent two eighth-century prophets — Isaiah and Micah — to
warn the nation.

Isaiah

Isaiah is the most important and influential of the "writing
prophets." The book that bears his name is the largest of all
prophetic books, and the New Testament quotes it more than
any other prophetic book.

We should look at the book of Isaiah as a collection of
prophecies that spanned perhaps 250 years. Chapters 1—39
come from the time of Isaiah of Jerusalem, the prophet who
preached from 742 B.C. to 700 B.C. Chapters 1—12 especially
bear the stamp of this son of Amoz. He preached a powerful
message of repentance to the southern kingdom.

Chapters 40—55 are the work of a compassionate anonymous prophet in the "school of Isaiah." He wrote around 550
B.C., toward the end of the Babylonian Captivity. These
chapters foretell the return to Jerusalem and a final recognition of all nations of the one true God. Known as *Second
Isaiah*, these chapters contain the beautiful Servant songs that
were so significant to Jesus' own ministry.

Finally, there is *Third Isaiah*, Chapters 56—66. Third Isaiah
was composed in Jerusalem after the Exile. It emphasizes the
place of the Temple and invites all nations to join the ranks of
Israel as God's Chosen People.

Sampling Isaiah

Please read Isaiah 1—7.

Chapter 1: List some sins of Judah.

2:4: What will happen in the future age?

3:16f: To what does Isaiah compare the nation?

5:1–7: Interpret this allegory.

**Outline of
First Isaiah (1—39)**

Chapters
1—12: Oracles against Judah
(740–732 B.C.)
13—23: Oracles against pagan nations (724–705 B.C.)
24—27: "Apocalypse" of Isaiah
28—33: Oracles from the last part of
Isaiah's ministry (705–700
B.C.)
34—35: A vision of Zion
36—39: Historical additions

■ *journal* ■

Compose your own version of the "Vineyard Song" (Is 5:1–7). Create an image for our nation and God in relationship to it. Does the nation need punishment? Why or why not?

Chapter 6: Read the notes in your Bible for this chapter. Because Isaiah's call took place in the Temple, some speculate that he may have been a priest. What signs and wonders accompanied his vocation?

How did he respond to God and how did God respond to him?

■

Who Was Isaiah?   Isaiah's life spanned the reigns of four kings — Uzziah, Jotham, Ahaz, and Hezekiah. Tradition holds that Hezekiah's son, Manasseh, killed the prophet, perhaps in 687 B.C.

Isaiah was a poet, a politician at ease in the kingly court, and a prophet of immense power. Chapter 6 tells us of the prophet's call in 742 B.C., the year of King Uzziah's death, a vision that shaped Isaiah's basic message.

At the Jerusalem Temple, Isaiah saw the Lord in a vision which revealed God's immense glory:

> Holy, holy, holy is Yahweh Sabaoth.
> His glory fills the whole earth (6:3).

This experience impressed on Isaiah his sinfulness before an all-holy God. God the creator was the majestic king of the universe and yet was also a king who humbly approached the Chosen People. Isaiah feared for his own life, believing that he, a mortal, would die after seeing God. But God purified him with a burning ember. This symbolized the purging of Isaiah's sins and God's commission to him to preach to an unrepentant, obstinate nation.

This encounter convinced Isaiah of God's holiness, a holiness the Chosen People must imitate by just living, true worship, and repenting of abuses that oppressed the poor and helpless. To Isaiah, Judah's basic problem was the pride of both the leaders and the people. They ignored the all-holy God and did not trust God completely. The prophet preached that a righteous God would punish Judah because of their stubbornness.

Repent!   We can divide Isaiah's message into three parts, each corresponding to the reign of a particular king: Jotham

(742–735 B.C), Ahaz (735–715 B.C.), and Hezekiah (715–687 B.C.). The earliest oracles (Chapters 1—5) correspond to the moral corruption of Judah and its capital during Jotham's reign. Isaiah indicted the nation for its many sins:

Idolatry: They have abandoned Yahweh, despised the Holy One of Israel, they have turned away from him (1:4).

Empty sacrifice: "What are your endless sacrifices to me?" says Yahweh. "I am sick of burnt offerings of rams and the fat of calves" (1:11).

Pride: Human pride will lower its eyes, human arrogance will be humbled, and Yahweh alone will be exalted, on that day (2:11).

Cruelty to the poor: "By what right do you crush my people and grind the faces of the poor?" says the Lord Yahweh Sabaoth (3:15).

In the face of this indictment, Isaiah calls people to repentance, a total commitment to God and to justice.

Take your wrong-doing out of my sight.
Cease doing evil. Learn to do good,
search for justice, discipline the violent,
be just to the orphan, plead for the widow (1:16–17).

Repentance would mend Judah's relationship with God. But Isaiah knew the people would not repent. God would have to judge and purify the nation. Isaiah prophesied God's chastisement of both Israel and Judah. He predicted a deportation of the people, first the northern kingdom to Assyria, then Judah to Babylon more than a century later.

In a beautiful story (5:1–7), Isaiah compared the nation to a vineyard that God cultivated. But because the vines refused to bear fruit, the vine dresser (God) had to prune it so a future generation might bear fruit.

Trust God Alone! The second phase of Isaiah's ministry took place during a complicated political situation. Economically, Judah was relatively prosperous, but this did not stop the rich from exploiting the poor. Politically, Assyria posed a serious threat, both to the northern kingdom and to the south. About 734 B.C., the kings of Damascus and Samaria in the north tried to convince Judah to join in a coalition against Assyria. But Judah and its king Ahaz decided to become a vassal to Assyria instead. This situation did not set well with Isaiah.

Ahaz foolishly sacrificed his son to false gods, hoping to ward off Assyria's threat. Isaiah attacked this colossal failure of faith. Because of Ahaz's foolishness it looked like the Davidic covenant would end with the death of Ahaz. But Isaiah promised a sign:

> The young woman is with child
> and will give birth to a son
> whom she will call Immanuel (7:14).

This son will have many names: "Wonder-Counsellor, Mighty-God, Eternal-Father, Prince-of-Peace" (9:5). These titles evoke the wisdom of Solomon, the valor and piety of David, and the many virtues of Moses and the patriarchs.

In Isaiah's day, a young woman did give birth to Ahaz's son, Hezekiah. And he did indeed become a religious king who tried to reform the traditional religion. But Christians see in Isaiah's prophecy about Immanuel, a name meaning "God is with us," a far more important reference to the promised Messiah, the Son of God, Jesus of Nazareth. Born of the virgin Mary (the term "young woman" was rendered *virgin* in the Greek translation of Isaiah), Jesus was king who would rule forever. And Jesus would accomplish God's will on earth as it is in heaven.

Hope. Despite the disobedience and infidelity of kings and despite the Chosen People's need to be purged of their sins, Isaiah offered a vision of hope. His prophecies included a future king who would obey Yahweh, and promised that God would save a "remnant" of the nation after the time of judgment.

This promise meant something to those living at the time of Hezekiah. Six years before he took power, Israel fell to Assyria. The leading citizens were deported; the northern kingdom ended. Hezekiah thought he could hold off Assyria by aligning Judah with Egypt, but again Isaiah condemned this action. Faith in Yahweh was Judah's only hope, not rebellion against Assyria.

In 701 B.C., the crafty Assyrian Sennacherib was on the march against Jerusalem. He sacked Judah's northern cities, and was poised ready to attack Jerusalem. Hezekiah's offer

• journal •

Read Is 9:1–6 and 11:1–9. These are messianic passages that the church applies to Jesus. But *Messiah* means "anointed one," a term that could be applied to any future king of Israel. How do these verses apply to Jesus? How does Isaiah envision the reign of this glorious king?

Part of a water tunnel built during Hezekiah's reign.

of gold from the Temple was not good enough. While the people waited in terror, Isaiah prayed to God. His message was that God would deliver the nation from Assyria's mighty hand. In fact, Assyria did retreat. 2 Kings 19:35 tells us that an angel visited the Assyrian camp and destroyed 185,000 soldiers. Sirach 48:21 records that a plague struck the Assyrian camp.

Yahweh spared Judah this time, but Isaiah prophesied that a new enemy — Babylon — would come into power after Hezekiah's death. This new power would punish Judah by taking Jerusalem, sacking the city, and carrying the people off to exile.

Hezekiah's son, Manasseh, turned out to be the worst of all Judah's kings. He went back to the worship of false gods and committed all kinds of atrocities. Manasseh's sins were the beginning of the fulfillment of Isaiah's prophecy.

But Isaiah's prophecies end on a hopeful note. Though God would use foreign nations as his instruments to punish an unrepentant nation, the Lord would also preserve a remnant. The Lord God will wipe away tears, smooth out the way of the just, revive the nation, and perform marvelous deeds.

> [On] that day the deaf
> will hear the words of the book
> and, delivered from shadow and darkness,
> the eyes of the blind will see.
> The lowly will find ever more joy in Yahweh
> and the poorest of people will delight in the Holy One
> of Israel;
> for the tyrant will be no more (Is 29:18–20).

■

Hezekiah's Reign

Please read the following passages from 2 Kings and answer the questions.

18:1–8: Was Hezekiah popular with the author of 2 Kings? Why or why not?

How old was Hezekiah when he came to power?

Chapter 19: Describe Sennacherib: _____

What does Isaiah prophesy?

Chapter 20: What does Isaiah prophesy concerning Babylon?

■

Micah

The prophet Micah was born in the lowly village of Moresheth in the Judean foothills. He preached at the same time as Isaiah of Jerusalem, during the reigns of Jotham, Ahaz, and Hezekiah. His images were drawn mostly from rural life. Micah's viewpoint was that of a peasant outraged by the injustices land owners committed against the poor.

Like Isaiah, and even more like Amos, Micah preached a message of judgment. Micah 1—3 condemns the leaders for their sins. The prophet directed his message to both kingdoms, calling them Jacob after the ancestor of the Israelites. He indicted leaders for hating good and loving evil. And Micah forcefully prophesied the destruction of Jerusalem and the Temple.

> That is why, thanks to you,
> Zion will become ploughland,
> Jerusalem a heap of rubble
> and the Temple Mount a wooded height (Mi 3:12).

However, like Isaiah, Micah told of a time when God would bring a universal reign of peace: "They will hammer their swords into ploughshares and their spears into billhooks" (Mi 4:3).

This same passage appears in Isaiah and thus shows a consistency in the messages of these two prophets. Micah also wrote of a messiah who would come to lead Israel to peace and justice. This anointed one will be from Bethlehem, a good shepherd who will rule by the strength of the Lord. He will gather *God's remnant*, a righteous group who would survive God's chastisement of the nation. This remnant will lead the nations to true worship of God.

You might want to memorize this well-known passage from Micah. It sums up the requirements of the Law and the Prophets: justice (Amos), loyal love (Hosea), and humble faith (Isaiah).

You have already been told what is right
and what Yahweh wants of you.
Only this, to do what is right,
to love loyalty
and to walk humbly with your God (Mi 6:8).

Jeremiah

Jeremiah was a towering Old Testament prophet. His message shouts the love of God, who desperately wanted the Chosen People to repent before catastrophe struck the nation. Jeremiah's own life testified as forcefully as his spoken words. His life had its ups and downs, drama, faith and doubts, struggles with God, suffering at the hands of kings, and loneliness.

God's dramatic involvement in Jeremiah's life prefigured the life of the greatest of all prophets, Jesus. Similarities between their lives abound: 1) both receive their vocation in their mother's womb (Jer 1:5, Lk 1:26–38); 2) their fellow citizens and family members reject them and their message (Jer 12:6, Lk 4:24–29); 3) both weep over Jerusalem (Jer 8:23, Lk 19:41); 4) both speak of a new covenant (Jer 31:31–33, Lk 22:20); 5) neither marries so they can devote themselves wholeheartedly to God's work; 6) the authorities torment both because of the truth of their message, a message that the leaders do not want to hear.

■

Sampling Jeremiah

Read the following selections from Jeremiah and answer the questions in your journal.

Chapter 5: What evils does Jeremiah describe? Why does the nation deserve punishment?

Chapter 7: Why is God not happy with the way worship is taking place?

Chapter 31: Does Jeremiah prophesy good news or bad news in this chapter? Explain.

Interpret the following "living symbols":

- 13:1–11 (loincloth)
- 18:1–12 (potter's vessel)
- 19:1–15 (smashed clay pot)

■

▪ *discuss* ▪

What does it mean for a teen today to —

- act justly
- love loyalty
- walk humbly with God

List five specific actions teens could realistically do for each of the above.

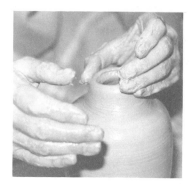

Living Parables. Jeremiah often enacted a living parable to deliver his messages. For example, Jeremiah never married, a rarity in the culture of his day. By this, he became a living symbol of the message that famine and slaughter would soon visit Jerusalem. This was no time to raise a family.

In another example, Jeremiah compared God to a potter. As a potter reshapes a flawed work, so Yahweh will mold the nation in his hands. In a dramatic gesture, Jeremiah shattered a jug in front of the elders and priests. This served to warn the nation that God would destroy those who had abandoned him.

After Babylon had already deported some captives (597 B.C.), Jeremiah walked through Jerusalem's streets with a wooden yoke on his shoulders to tell the people that only by submitting to Babylon could Judah escape destruction. The false prophets hated Jeremiah's message, so they told the people what they wanted to hear, that they would never become slaves of Babylon. Time proved Jeremiah the true prophet.

Though Jeremiah delivered a message of doom that his contemporaries did not want to hear, he also looked beyond the tragedy to a new day. For example, even while Judah was under siege by the Babylonians in the fateful year of 587 B.C., Jeremiah bought a field. Despite the bleakness of the present moment, God has a future for Judah: the God of the covenant will bring joy and prosperity to the land and an ideal king will rule in the future.

The Writings. The book of Jeremiah is a mixture of many literary forms: history and biography, poetry and prose, enacted parables, lament and prophecy. Unfortunately, the book does not have a chronological order. Rather, the editors arranged the material thematically, drawing on booklets of Jeremiah's original words, sermons based on his words, biographical materials written by his secretary, Baruch, and traditions handed on by his disciples.

The Message. Scholars note many similarities between Jeremiah's basic themes and those of the prophet Hosea and Deuteronomist authors, particularly the covenant and sin and repentance.

Outline of Jeremiah

- Oracles in the days of King Josiah (Ch 1—6)
- Oracles in the days of King Jehoiakim (Ch 7—20)
- Oracles in Jerusalem's last years (Ch 21—33)
- Fall of Jerusalem (Ch 34—45)
- Oracles against the nations (Ch 46—51)
- Historical appendix (Ch 52)

Jeremiah repeatedly warned that the people's sins would lead to sorrow and punishment. God had been so good to them (Jer 2), but they had rebelled. If they would amend their behavior, however, God would withhold his avenging hand.

> "If you really amend your behavior and your actions, if you really treat one another fairly, if you do not exploit the stranger, the orphan and the widow, if you do not shed innocent blood in this place and if you do not follow other gods, to your own ruin, then I shall let you stay in this place, in the country I gave for ever to your ancestors of old" (Jer 7:5–7).

But no one listened to Jeremiah. His urgent message fell on deaf ears. He warned time and again of a foe from the north who would destroy Jerusalem and carry the people off into exile. Despite God's chastisement, Jeremiah still gave rays of hope. Beyond the punishment, God would restore the nation.

Jeremiah 30—33 offers a message of encouragement and consolation. The people were already in Babylon, but he had good news for them. God would establish a new covenant:

> "Look, the days are coming, Yahweh declares, when I shall make a new covenant with the House of Israel (and the House of Judah), but not like the covenant I made with their ancestors. . . . Within them I shall plant my Law, writing it on their hearts. Then I shall be their God and they will be my people. . . . They will all know me, from the least to the greatest, Yahweh declares, since I shall forgive their guilt and never more call their sin to mind" (Jer 31:31–34).

This passage gave much hope to the suffering Chosen People. God will take the initiative by giving people new hearts so they will be obedient to the Lord. The new covenant will change them. Knowledge of God will be from within; it will be personal. It will no longer only be written on tablets of stone (as in Exodus) or in law books (as in Deuteronomy). God will touch a person's heart so the Lord may live within.

Jeremiah's new covenant is closely tied to the covenant God made through Moses on Mount Sinai. The God of the Sinai covenant was already compassionate and forgiving. The uniqueness of the new covenant is not found in its

Archbishop Oscar Romero of El Salvador, a contemporary prophet

■ *journal* ■

Read Jer 20:7–18. Write your own "confession" to the Lord of a time when you were upset with what he asked of you. State your own faith in the God who will always stay by your side.

terms, which are the same as those of Sinai. What is new is that the ability to obey the covenant is now given internally, written on the heart of each person. Thus the permanence of the covenant is assured.

Christians have read these words of Jeremiah as a prophecy of the covenant established by Jesus. The Savior's life, death, and resurrection inaugurates the new covenant. It is a sign of God's grace, heals and conquers our sin, and pours out new life and the precious gift of the Holy Spirit.

Faith.   Jeremiah suffered much for Yahweh. He did not want to be a prophet and hated delivering a message that people did not want to hear. His brothers attacked him. His fellow citizens thought he was a traitor. The leaders wished to do away with him. He came to the brink of despair:

> A disaster for me, mother, that you bore me
> to be a man of strife and dissension for the whole
>   country (15:10).

He complained to God and begged for help:

> Do not be a terror to me,
> you, my refuge in time of disaster.
> Let my persecutors be confounded, not me (17:17–18).

In total honesty, he reproached God. In his anger, he criticized God:

> You have seduced me, Yahweh, and I have let myself be
>   seduced;
> you have overpowered me: you were the stronger.
> I am a laughing-stock all day long,
> they all make fun of me (20:7).

Jeremiah did not want to continue speaking in God's name because of all the suffering it brought him, but he could not help himself. There was "a fire burning in [his] heart, imprisoned in [his] bones" that forced him to speak on God's behalf. Despite his personal suffering and reluctance, Jeremiah remained faithful to God. Jeremiah's words remind us that, despite all obstacles to speak and work for truth, God will never desert us: "But Yahweh is at my side like a mighty hero" (Jer 20:11).

The Book of Lamentations.   The Greek Bible places this book of five poetic laments after the book of Jeremiah.

Scholars doubt that Jeremiah wrote them, since both the content and style differ from Jeremiah.

These heart-wrenching poems mournfully lament the destruction of Jerusalem and the Temple, a symbol that God had abandoned them. Today's Jews still read Lamentations aloud in synagogues in mid-July to recall the anniversary of the destruction of the Temple in 587 B.C. and the later destruction in A.D. 70.

• *journal* •

Read the first chapter of Lamentations. Transcribe into your journal the verse that strikes you as the saddest.

A Look at the Minor Prophets

Baruch. Though the book derives its name from Jeremiah's secretary, who plays an important role in Jer 36—45, an anonymous author or authors wrote Baruch between the second and first century B.C. Drawing on the work of Jeremiah, Baruch borrows themes from the Babylonian Exile to encourage the people of its own and later times to repent and look to a day when they could return to their land. Baruch encourages Jews of its day to remain firm in faith and to resist adopting Greek ways.

Other prophets proclaimed God's word during these extraordinary years of Judah's history. Here is a brief sketch of three of them.

Zephaniah

Who? A fiery preacher who may have been a prophet attached to the Temple and may have thundered his prophecies during Temple liturgies.

When? The early days of King Josiah's reign, perhaps between 640–625 B.C. (shortly before Jeremiah).

Nahum

Who? A little-known prophet who uttered a strong prophecy against Nineveh, the hated capital of Assyria.

When? Shortly before the fall of Nineveh to the Babylonians in 612 B.C.

Habakkuk

Who? Probably a prophet attached to the Temple who lived shortly after Nahum during Jehoiakim's reign (609–598 B.C.).

When? Wrote when Babylon was conquering the Near East (c. 600 B.C.), while Judah was floundering under a corrupt king.

Zephaniah

What? Predicts a "day of the Lord," when sinners will be punished; also preaches the good news that the Lord will spare a "holy remnant" on whom God will build a new nation.

Key verse: "The great Day of Yahweh is near, near, and coming with great speed. That Day is a day of retribution, a day of distress and tribulation" (Zep 1:14a, 15a).

Nahum

What? A "battle curse" that depicts God as an avenger; though the book gloats over the fury of an avenging God, the Chosen People would have taken heart in a God who protects them from their enemies.

Key verse: "Yahweh is slow to anger but great in power, Yahweh never lets evil go unpunished" (Na 1:3).

Habakkuk

What? The prophet complains to God that an idolatrous Judah was escaping punishment; Yahweh replies that Babylon will be his instrument to punish Judah; the Lord will save the righteous, those who believe in God.

Key verse: "You see, anyone whose heart is not upright will succumb, but the upright will live through faithfulness" (Hb 2:4).

▪ *class project* ▪

Divide into nine groups, each group taking one of the chapters from these books. Prepare and deliver a brief report of the content of your assigned chapter.

Ezekiel

Ezekiel's bizarre behavior, fantastic visions, striking symbolic actions, and prophetic utterances challenge Bible scholars even today. Despite our inability to comprehend this controversial prophet fully, the themes he preaches are clear.

Ezekiel was born into a priestly family. He was probably among those aristocratic Jews that Nebuchadnezzar, king of Babylonia, deported in 597 B.C., after the siege of Jerusalem. He settled at Tel-Abib, a canal town near the Euphrates River southeast of Babylon.

His Call. The book of Ezekiel carefully dates his prophetic call and ministry. In 593 B.C., at the age of thirty, Ezekiel had a fantastic vision of God (Ez 1). He saw a chariot drawn by four winged creatures, each having four faces that represent attributes of God: courage (lion), strength (ox), swiftness (eagle), intelligence (man). This vision struck Ezekiel dumb. Eventually, God's voice instructed him to eat a scroll. The scroll, which contained God's word, tasted as sweet as honey, but the message it held would fall on the deaf ears of a stubborn people.

His Message Before the Fall of Jerusalem.   The first part of Ezekiel's ministry took place in Babylon before the fall of Jerusalem in 587 B.C. During these years, Ezekiel censured the people of God (Chapters 3—24) and the nations (Chapters 25—32) for their sinful conduct. Through his prophetic words and actions, he tried to stir the people to repent before doom struck the nation.

We find a particularly stirring action in Ezekiel 5. Ezekiel built a model of Jerusalem, and then cursed it. He then cut off all the hair from his face and head (a most bizarre act for a Jewish man of his day) and divided it into three parts. He burned the first part of his hair, chopped up the second part, and threw the third to the wind, pursuing it with a sword. The hair represented the inhabitants of Jerusalem. Fire would destroy a third of them during a protracted siege of the city. Another third would die by the sword, while a final third would be scattered into exile. From the latter portion, the prophet took a few hairs, to represent a remnant the Lord would save to rebuild the nation.

▪ *journal* ▪

Answer the following questions in your journal.

Read Ezekiel 1—3:

1. Describe or sketch a drawing of Ezekiel's vision of Yahweh's chariot.
2. Briefly note what else happens to Ezekiel. What is his function supposed to be (3:16–17)?

Read Ez 4—5: What is the purpose of these symbolic actions?

In another symbolic action, Ezekiel planned an elaborate escape from the city by digging through a wall at night. He warned that this pantomime represented King Zedekiah's future attempt to escape the Babylonian siege of Jerusalem. But the Babylonians would capture and blind him and send him to exile to die. Despite Ezekiel's elaborate and shocking

Reproduction of the ancient Babylonian Ishtar Gate

■ *journal* ■

Please read Ez 34:1–25. To whom do Christians apply this passage? Why?

behavior, the people still refused to repent. The Lord instructed Ezekiel to tell the people: "There will be no further delay in the fulfilling of any of my words. What I have said shall be done now" (Ez 12:28).

Like all prophets, Ezekiel suffered ridicule and rejection for his message. The worst affront was that people simply ignored his message. They could not imagine that God would destroy Jerusalem considering the promises made to David. But the Lord vindicated Ezekiel's message: Jerusalem fell; the king was carried off to exile.

"My people sit down in front of you and listen to your words, but they do not act on them.... As far as they are concerned, you are like a love song pleasantly sung to a good musical accompaniment. They listen to your words, but no one acts on them. When the thing takes place — and it is beginning now — they will know that there has been a prophet among them" (Ez 33:31–33).

Ezekiel's Message After the Fall of Jerusalem.   The tone of Ezekiel's prophecies changed radically after he received notice of Jerusalem's fall. A demoralized, defeated nation joined him in exile. God's prophet did not desert them but instead changed his message to one of hope and consolation.

Chapters 33—39 include the promise of a new king, a shepherd who will make a covenant of peace with the people. These chapters also predict a time when God would restore the nation. Ezekiel also reported a dream of standing in a field of dry bones, a prophetic dream that gave great hope to the nation:

"These bones are the whole House of Israel.... The Lord Yahweh says this: I am now going to open your graves; I shall raise you from your graves, my people, and lead you back to the soil of Israel. And you will know that I am Yahweh, when I open your graves and raise you from your graves, my people, and put my spirit in you, and you revive, and I resettle you on your own soil. Then you will know that I, Yahweh, have spoken and done this" (Ez 37:11–14).

The final chapters of Ezekiel (40—48) also end on a hopeful note. The prophet tells of the building of a new Temple, a new Jerusalem, and the nation's return.

Ezekiel's Influence.   Several themes dominate the theology of Ezekiel. Like other prophets, he stressed God's awesome holiness, protested the people's sin, and called for repentance. As a priest, he also underscored the need to keep the covenant through worship of God. We discover an emphasis on regulations and rituals not present in the works of the other prophets. He called on the people to repent of profaning the Sabbath day, of worshiping on high places, and of defiling the sanctuary. The Law of Holiness of Leviticus (17—26) had a profound influence on his thinking. He significantly influenced the Judaism that emerged after the Exile.

Ezekiel also stressed the important theme of individual responsibility. Contrary to popular teaching of his day, Ezekiel proclaimed that God is a just God. The Lord does not punish one generation for the sins of another. Everyone is accountable for his or her sins.

Ezekiel prophesied until perhaps 573 B.C. He died in Exile, but his message lived on to give hope and consolation to the exiled nation. In our next chapter, we will see how Yahweh did indeed restore the exiles to their homeland, to the holy city, and to the Temple. The eccentric Ezekiel had condemned an unrepentant nation, but, more important, he offered the hope of a future vision. God surely punished sinners, but did so to save the people. Ezekiel's final message was one of hope.

Artist's conception of ancient Babylon

Reading Ezekiel

Read Ezekiel 18. Answer the following questions in your journal.

1. What is the meaning of the proverb in verse 2?

2. Will God punish a son for his father's crimes (v. 20)? Why or why not?

3. Which verse tells us that God will save a wicked person who repents of his or her past sins?

4. What are some of the standards God wants us to follow (see vv. 5–9, 14–17)?

▪ *focus questions* ▪

1. What were the major religious problems in the southern kingdom between 922–721 B.C.?

▪ *journal* ▪

Read Ez 34 and Jn 10:1–21. Contrast the traits of a bad shepherd with those of a good shepherd. How is Jesus the "Good Shepherd"?

2. Identify Isaiah of Jerusalem. Discuss a key theme of his preaching.

3. Distinguish among First Isaiah, Second Isaiah, and Third Isaiah.

4. Explain what prophets such as Isaiah meant by *repentance*.

5. Who was King Ahaz? What important prophecy did Isaiah make about his dynasty?

6. Identify *the remnant*.

7. What significant event in the history of Judah took place in 701 B.C.?

8. What did King Manasseh do that led to the fall of Judah?

9. What verse from Micah sums up the heart of his message?

10. Describe in detail one of the living parables of Jeremiah.

11. Why is Jeremiah known as a "prophet of doom"?

12. What did Jeremiah mean by a "new covenant"?

13. How is Jeremiah a symbol of faith?

14. Why was Lamentations written?

15. Briefly comment on the messages of the following books: Baruch, Zephaniah, Nahum, and Habakkuk.

16. Who was Ezekiel?

17. Discuss the twofold aspect of Ezekiel's message.

18. Interpret Ezekiel's vision of the dry bones. Would this bring hope or despair to the people?

19. In general, do you see the prophets preaching a message of doom or of hope or of both? Explain.

20. Briefly identify:

Sennacherib	Nebuchadnezzar
King Hezekiah	Baruch

▪ *exercise* ▪

In the style of Jeremiah or Ezekiel, outline a small pantomime or skit that would prophetically call attention to the immorality of one of the following contemporary social issues:

abortion	consumerism
poverty	arms build-up
environmental pollution	prejudice

▪ *vocabulary* ▪

Copy the meaning of the following words into the vocabulary section of your journal:

bemoan	indictment
censure	lamentation
chastisement	

Prayer Reflection

Psalms 42–43 are actually a single poem, a lament in which the psalmist in Exile yearns for a return to the Temple. The first two verses speak for anyone who longs to be close to God. Make these words your words.

> As a deer yearns
>   for running streams,
> so I yearn
>   for you, my God.
> I thirst for God,
>   the living God;
> when shall I go to see
>   the face of God?
>
> — Psalm 42:1–2

■ *reflection* ■

What do you most hope for in your life right now? How does it compare to friendship with our loving God?

■ *resolution* ■

The psalmist bemoans the fact that he is away from the Temple and cannot visit God in the sanctuary. This is not the case with us. We can visit Jesus in the tabernacle whenever we pass by a church or chapel. Why not stop by and visit the Lord for fifteen minutes one day this week? Tell him about your day, what he means to you, what your real desires are. Ask him to be living water for you.

chapter 8

Rebuilding
After the Exile

Is not this the sort of fast that pleases me:
...to let the oppressed go free?...
Is it not sharing your food with the hungry,
and sheltering the homeless poor;
if you see someone lacking clothes, to clothe him,
and not to turn away from your own kin?
Then your light will blaze out like the dawn.

— Isaiah 58:6–8a

Look carefully at these words:

"That that is is that that is not is not is not that it it is."

What can you make of this? It looks like nonsense. But don't despair. Proper punctuation will make the meaning clear.

"That that is, is; that that is not, is not! Is not that it? It is."

Like this sentence, the story of God's Chosen People may appear at first glance to be somewhat meaningless. The many ups and downs, fidelities and infidelities, victories and inevitable defeats may strike us as unintelligible. What is God trying to say and accomplish in his dealings with the Chosen People? Prophets, priests, scribes, and holy people have discerned God working in the history of this unique people, a God who "writes straight with crooked lines." God's revelation in the Hebrew scriptures clarifies apparent chaos.

For example, the tragedy of the Babylonian Captivity served to purge the people. Prophets such as Second Isaiah saw God's activity even in the midst of a setback — he kept alive the hope that Yahweh would save the people and taught that suffering brings redemption. The Old Testament repeatedly shouts the exclamation point of God's love for the Chosen People.

To Witness or Not to Witness?

The book of Jonah derives its name from an eighth century B.C. prophet (see 2 Kgs 14:25), but it is not his work. The story is set in Nineveh, the sinful capital of Assyria. The author of the parable writes freely of God's love for and forgiveness of everyone, including hated enemies such as Assyria.

Many scholars date the book from the late fifth century B.C., after the Exile. Some leading Jews, including Ezra and Nehemiah, emphasized the need for Jews to keep to themselves. Such teaching can lead to exclusivism and nationalism. The purpose of Jonah is to remind us that God's love is universal, meant for all nations.

1. *Read* Jonah.

2. *Reflect on the following questions.*

   a. Are you willing to share your Christian faith with others?

   > Yes   No   Uncertain

   b. Rate how difficult you find it to forgive your enemies:

   Impossible   Difficult   Somewhat difficult   I can do it

   c. What does *Nineveh* symbolize in your own life? Check one:

   _____ a difficult assignment
   _____ unpleasant classmates
   _____ an emotion I don't want to deal with
   _____ a bad habit

   d. What is God asking of you in your life right now?

   e. Who or what might be speaking this word of God to you?

   f. What is your response to God's request?

   _____ I am taking steps to obey it.
   _____ I am ignoring it.
   _____ I am going in the opposite direction.

. journal .

Write of a time when you disobeyed the request of a legitimate authority figure, but later repented of your disobedience. What did you learn from this experience?

. discuss .

What message should teens be speaking to the Ninevehs in today's world. What are the most effective ways to do it?

The Chosen People in Exile

Nebuchadnezzar's destruction of Jerusalem (587 B.C.) and his deportations to Babylon began a new phase in the story of the Chosen People. Those who remained in Palestine were helpless, weak, leaderless, and without direction. Others fled to Egypt for safety and established small settlements on the Nile. The ones who were deported to Babylon — perhaps between 12,000 and 16,000 of them — settled in villages and small rural communities, many along the Chebar Canal, which flowed out of Babylon itself. The Jewish exiles had a decent life in their new land, participating in its commercial, agricultural, and cultural life. Jeremiah even encouraged them to try to live as normally as possible. Indeed, ancient records reveal that some Jewish families flourished.

Despite the freedoms permitted, for the pious Jew living in exile Babylon was still a foreign land, unclean in God's eyes. Observant Jews longed for the day when Yahweh would permit them to return to Jerusalem. Their major challenge was to prevent intermarriage and assimilation into the conquering people, which would lead to the loss of identity as a separate people. This happened to the Israelites deported by the Assyrians in the eighth century B.C.

To separate themselves from their captors, the exiles engaged in activities that stamped them as a special people — circumcision, Sabbath observance, and study of the Law. There was no temple or proper place for sacrifices, so they gathered in synagogues (prayer-houses), where they studied and prayed together. In these assemblies, scribes collected Israel's oral traditions and wrote them down as a permanent record of how God dealt with his people. Many of these texts became the sacred scriptures, and reminded future generations of God's many blessings on the people and divine punishments for disobedience.

Through this era's prophetic voices — Jeremiah, Ezekiel, and Second Isaiah — the people learned of God's plan to preserve a remnant of the people. This remnant in exile was to learn from the past so they could return to Jerusalem and renew the covenant with Yahweh. We find heartfelt feelings of the exiles expressed in psalms written during this time.

■ *journal* ■

Read Isaiah 40—44. Transcribe in your journal at least five verses that speak of God's mercy and tenderness to the Chosen People.

For example, Psalm 74 and Psalm 79 lament the destruction of the Temple. Psalm 102 begs God to help the people who are suffering such misfortune. Psalm 137 petitions Yahweh to seek revenge on Babylon.

Let us turn now to the most consoling voice of the Exile, the prophet known as Second Isaiah.

Second Isaiah

The author of Isaiah 40—55 is anonymous. He wrote in the spirit of the prophet Isaiah, perhaps around 550 B.C. His hope-filled message, framed in masterful poetry, is among the most beloved in the Hebrew scriptures.

Also known as Isaiah of Babylon, he encouraged his Jewish brothers and sisters in exile when the Babylonian empire was on the verge of collapse. He saw clearly that a new kingdom was on the rise — Persia — and that its tolerant leader Cyrus would serve as God's instrument to free the Jews. Cyrus did indeed conquer Babylon and then, in 538 B.C., issued an Edict of Toleration, permitting exiled peoples to return home. It also allowed them to restore their religious shrines. This important date in Jewish history marked the time when God's remnant began the journey back to Jerusalem.

When Isaiah of Babylon wrote, the Jews had been in exile for forty years and were certain that God had abandoned them in this strange land. Many of the original exiles had died. A new generation had been born, but Israel still suffered humiliation. To his fellow exiles, the prophet offered a message of comfort and salvation. Let us take a look at some of the key themes in his work, known as the Book of Consolation.

Key Themes. Second Isaiah opens his work with a message of consolation for a suffering people. God instructed him to tell the people that Israel had paid the price for its sins.

> "Console my people, console them,"
> says your God.
> "Speak to the heart of Jerusalem
> and cry to her
> that her period of service is ended,
> that her guilt has been atoned for" (Is 40:1–2a).

The prophet proclaims an important message — God is coming to save his people:

> A voice cries, "Prepare in the desert
> a way for Yahweh.
> Make a straight highway for our God
> across the wastelands.
> Let every valley be filled in,
> every mountain and hill be levelled,
> every cliff become a plateau,
> every escarpment a plain;
> then the glory of Yahweh will be revealed" (Is 40:3–5a).

The prophet reassures the people that God loves them deeply. In a male-oriented world, the prophet could write of the love of God as that of a mother for her baby:

> Can a woman forget her baby at the breast,
> feel no pity for the child she has borne?
> Even if these were to forget,
> I shall not forget you.
> Look, I have engraved you on the palms of my hands
> (Is 49:15–16a).

A dominant theme in Second Isaiah is God's promise to send a messiah to lead the Chosen People in a new exodus. The Lord's instrument will be Cyrus of Persia (Is 45:1).

Second Isaiah has a reassuring message of deliverance and hope, but he also teaches that God is the one, all-powerful, creator God. The prophet forcefully states that all that exists comes from, depends on, and is subject to God:

> I am the first and I am the last;
> there is no God except me (Is 44:6b).

> I am Yahweh, and there is no other,
> I form the light and I create the darkness,
> I make well-being, and I create disaster,
> I, Yahweh, do all these things (45:6b–7).

This unique God singled out the Israelites for a specific task: They must serve as a beacon to attract other nations to the worship of the one true God: "I shall make you a light to the nations so that my salvation may reach the remotest parts of earth" (Is 49:6). The Lord wants nothing less than for all people at all times to recognize who he is and what he deserves:

■ *journal* ■

What does a mother's love mean to you? How is God's love like that of a mother?

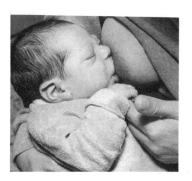

■ *discuss* ■

Should the church present more forcefully the imagery of God as mother? Explain.

> All shall bend the knee to me,
> by me every tongue shall swear,
> saying, "In Yahweh alone
> are saving justice and strength,"
> until all those who used to rage at him
> come to him in shame (Is 45:23b–24).

Servant of God. Second Isaiah contains four distinct poems that deal with a specific individual, "the servant," whom God will use to usher in a glorious future.

Scholars do not agree on the identity of this servant. One theory holds that the servant is a personification of the nation of Israel, a composite picture of Israel's ideal people, those who embody the true values of the nation. Another theory suggests the servant is the prophet himself or someone like Jeremiah. Christians see in these servant passages prophetic images of Jesus, the servant whose suffering redeemed all people.

The Babylonian Isaiah may have had in mind someone who would embody the true values and faith of the Jewish people. Through him, God would accomplish the divine will both for the Chosen People and the entire world. The servant is never called *Messiah*, but Christians believe Jesus applied these passages to himself. Jesus uniquely interpreted the messianic way to salvation as the path of suffering and service.

The Message of the Servant Songs. The first song (42:1–4) speaks of God's chosen one who has God's spirit. Gently, he will bring justice to the world and treat the bruised reed, Israel, tenderly.

The second song (49:1–6) tells how God chose the servant before his birth. The servant's strength is his prophetic word — "a sharp-edged sword" — which will bring spiritual light and salvation to the nations.

The third song (50:4–9) describes how God's special messenger runs into resentment. People beat and spit on him and pluck his beard. Yet the servant suffers quietly. He knows that God will vindicate him and that his enemies will disintegrate, like moth-eaten cloth.

The final song (52:13—53:12) has remarkable parallels to Jesus Christ's suffering, death, and resurrection. The servant, perhaps representing Israel, is brutally treated. He is like a lamb led to slaughter, the one God chose to bear the guilt of

■ *journal* ■

Read Isaiah 52:13—53:12.
Note three ways this passage applies to Jesus.
Reflect on how you are an instrument of God's love.

■ *journal* ■

Read Mt 12:17–21. How did Matthew see Jesus?

the world's sins. Without complaint, the servant accepts a painful, humiliating death, so that through him the world can be saved.

These magnificent servant songs stress God's love for all people. Isaiah of Babylon delivered one of the Hebrew scriptures' most important messages: *the one, the almighty creator God is a saving God who forgives and forgets*:

> As for foreigners who ... cling to my covenant:
> these I shall lead to my holy mountain....
> [And] my house will be called a house of prayer for all
> peoples (Is 56:6–7).

The Return

Ranking among the important events in Jewish history was the restoration to the Promised Land after sixty years in exile. The people who returned to Judah (over 40,000 according to the book of Ezra) had undergone a conversion.

The Babylonian conquest destroyed Solomon's Temple, and put an end to the monarchy and centuries of political independence. The Exile taught the Chosen People an important lesson: God would not tolerate idolatry and pagan worship. After the restoration, purified Judaism would be more conscious of and faithful to its vocation of witnessing to the nations by keeping the Law.

Many Obstacles.   The returning Jews, led by Zerubbabel, a descendent of King David, and the priest Joshua, faced many obstacles. They had three major tasks before them: 1) rebuild the Temple; 2) rebuild Jerusalem and its walls; 3) re-establish the worship of Yahweh and renew the Mosaic covenant.

Presenting a major obstacle to harmonious resettlement were the Samaritans. They were a mixed population of Israelites of the northern kingdom who intermarried with foreigners from Assyria. They worshiped God at the sanctuaries at Dan and Bethel. Although the Samaritans wanted to help rebuild the Temple, the returning Jews distrusted them and refused their help. Mutual distrust would fester between Jews and Samaritans for generations.

During the period of restoration many exiles remained in Babylon, Egypt, and elsewhere. They looked to Jerusalem for leadership, paid taxes to the Temple, and made pilgrimages to the holy city. However, these Jews were more open to the influence of Gentile ideas not always appreciated by the Jews in Israel.

A Changed Religion.   Judaism would never be the same as it was before the Exile. More Jews lived outside Palestine than within. The synagogue became an important institution for Jewish communities outside Israel. *Rabbis*, teachers of the Law, and *scribes* who copied and interpreted sacred scriptures, became increasingly important religious roles both within and outside Israel.

The decades after the return were a time of consolidation, reflection, and recommitment. Key prophets of this era — for example, Haggai, Zechariah, and Malachi — wrote about issues such as the rebuilding of the Temple, the role of priests, and proper worship. They wanted to strengthen Jewish identity. They also prophesied about the universal appeal of Jewish faith and the salvation God would bring to all people through an "anointed one."

Strong personalities such as Nehemiah, the Persian-appointed governor of Judah, and Ezra, the reformer-scribe, helped create post-exilic Judaism. Nehemiah saw to the rebuilding of Jerusalem. Ezra led the people to a renewal of the covenant, an event celebrated by the reading of the Law and the celebration of the feasts of Tabernacles and Day of Atonement. He saw the Jews as a holy race, a consecrated nation who would lead others to God.

During this period of restoration, the Hebrew scriptures took on their present form. Scribes compiled and edited the earlier texts and oral traditions. The Pentateuch was completed and the older historical books reached their final form. Editors collected and organized the works of the prophets. This period also produced some original writings of its own, most notably the historical books of Chronicles and Ezra-Nehemiah and the prophetic books of Haggai, Zechariah, Third Isaiah, Joel, Obadiah, Jonah, and Malachi. We will introduce some of the key themes of these books below.

Chronicles, Ezra, Nehemiah

Chronicles.   Both books of Chronicles once formed a single work with Ezra and Nehemiah. The author of Chronicles was a priest from Jerusalem who probably wrote sometime in the fourth century B.C., perhaps around 350. He sought to write a sacred history that focused on the Jews as a priestly people. He studied the other historical books and extracted from them the materials that stressed his two main religious themes: true worship and true kingship in Israel.

This author's job was to link his generation with the past. The Chronicler believed the key insight of Jewish identity was its role as priests, a community of people through whom Yahweh would instruct all nations. Thus, these books stress true worship of God and the important role of the priests and Levites in Temple worship.

Chronicles also forcefully instructed the post-exilic generation to learn from history. The nation's happiness depends on true fidelity to God. God is faithful to his covenants. He even miraculously rescues his people. However, God also punishes idolatry and disobedience of the Law, as the history of both the northern and southern kingdoms showed.

Chronicles highlights the nation of Judah, portraying it as more faithful to the covenant than the northern kingdom. It focuses on the kingships of David and Solomon, ideal kings in the eyes of the Chronicler because they centered Israelite worship in Jerusalem and its Temple and prodded the people to be faithful to God. The current generation should strive for fidelity in worship of the one true God. It should also be ever watchful or punishment would once again befall the nation.

Ezra and Nehemiah. These books were originally one book, though we are not sure of the chronology of the events reported in them. The present order of the books assumes Ezra came first, probably because he was the most prominent post-exilic Jew, credited with restoring Jewish life after the Exile. Historically, Nehemiah probably came first, rebuilding Jerusalem and introducing some religious reforms, after which Ezra came to re-establish the faith of the people.

The book of Ezra begins with Cyrus of Persia's decree to let the Jews return home. Ezra 1—6 tells us about the first two groups of exiles returning home, one led by Sheshbazzar (in 538 B.C.) and another by Zerubbabel (around 520 B.C.). These chapters also relate some of the problems the returning Jews met in trying to rebuild the Temple. "The enemies of Judah" and "the people of the land" tried to convince the Persians that the restoration of Jerusalem was a treasonous act. Their opposition, however, crumbled as the Temple was completed in 515 B.C., largely through the urging of the

Outline of 1–2 Chronicles, Ezra-Nehemiah

1 Chr 1—9	Genealogies from Adam to after the Exile
1 Chr 10—29	David's reign
2 Chr 1—9	Solomon's reign
2 Chr 10—36	Judah's kings to the Exile
Ezr 1—6	Early exiles return
Ezr 7—10	Ezra and his reforms
Neh 1—7	Nehemiah and the Jerusalem walls
Neh 8—10	Covenant renewal ceremony
Neh 11—13	The nation reformed

■ *journal* ■

Read Ezr 1; 3–5; 7:1–10; 9:1–15. **Answer the following questions in your journal.**

1. **What did the Samaritans do to hamper the rebuilding of the Temple?**
2. **Who was Ezra?**
3. **What does Ezra forbid?**

prophets Haggai and Zechariah. This temple, however, lacked the splendor of Solomon's Temple.

The first seven and last three chapters of Nehemiah tell of a remarkable public servant, Nehemiah. Around 445 B.C. he persuaded the Persian king Artaxerxes I to make him governor of Judah. Nehemiah then proceeded, against Samaritan opposition, to rebuild the walls of Jerusalem. This feat symbolized the autonomy of the Jewish nation and its reestablishment in the Promised Land. Nehemiah served two twelve-year terms, from 445–433 B.C. and again from 430–417 B.C.

Many scholars believe that Ezra came to Jerusalem during the reign of the Persian king Artaxerxes II, perhaps in 398 B.C. Ezra was a priest and a great religious reformer. Ezra 7—10 tells of his mission. An expert in the Torah (Law), he set about to vigorously reform the Jewish faith.

First, he forbade mixed marriages and dissolved Jewish marriages with non-Jews. Second, he forbade unnecessary mingling with foreign nations. His intent here was to establish the purity of the Jews as God's holy people. He was concerned with the survival of the Jewish nation. He unified them and gave them a spiritual vision that helped preserve them as a distinct religion.

Nehemiah 8—10 describes Ezra's greatest achievement — the promulgation of the Torah. Ezra read the Law. The people of Jerusalem confessed their failure to live the Law. Finally, the people rededicated themselves to the Law and promised to observe its precepts. Ezra established the Torah as the constitution of Judaism. Fidelity to the Torah set the spiritual tone of the post-exilic Jewish community and helped Judaism survive to our own day.

Prophets of the Return

Haggai: The Temple. Haggai's prophetic activity took place in 520 B.C., about two decades after the return. He exhorts his fellow Jews to rebuild the Temple, linking the poverty, drought, and crop failure suffered by his countrymen to their thoughtless concern about rebuilding their own houses while neglecting God's house.

Zechariah: Messianic Age to Come. The first eight chapters of the book of Zechariah belong to a prophet who preached from 520–518 B.C. The last six chapters belong to an anony-

■ *journal* ■

Read Neh 2; 8—10. Answer the following questions in your journal.

1. Who rebuilt Jerusalem?
2. What are the key points of Ezra's prayer in Neh 9:6–37?
3. What are some key provisions of the pact made by the people in Neh 10?

■ *journal* ■

Read Haggai and answer the following questions.

1:1–11 Which verse tells us why the Jews are suffering?
1:12–15 Who is responsible for rebuilding the Temple?
2:3–9 Does the Temple compare favorably with the old? What will the Lord do about it?

mous prophet who delivered his oracles against the Greeks 150 years later.

Zechariah 1—8 delivers the same basic message as Haggai. The prophet wants to rebuild the Temple and build a purified community. He also predicts a Messianic age to come. As the son of a priest, Zechariah emphasizes the role of the high priest, Joshua, more than Haggai does.

Third Isaiah: Light to the Nations. Isaiah 56—66 contains a mixture of poetry and prose oracles composed by a disciple or disciples of Isaiah of Babylon shortly after the return from the Exile. These chapters present a mixed message of hope and gloom. The message of hope comes in prophetic visions of a revitalized Israel. It looks to a future day when God's light will shine on the Jewish nation and attract all people to God. God promises:

> I will make you an object of eternal pride,
> a source of joy from age to age (Is 60:15).

The vocation of a restored Jerusalem would be lofty: to bring glad tidings to the lowly, heal the brokenhearted, proclaim liberty to captives, release to prisoners, and to comfort those who mourn (cf. Is 61:1–3).

On the dark side, the prophets saw the cold reality facing the returning exiles: a city that was a pale image of its former self; a stubborn people who resisted change, especially the Samaritans, who occupied the land; economic ruin; lackluster religious faith that did not translate into deeds of love and mercy for the poor and helpless. In Third Isaiah, we see some of the same fiery call to repentance that was the vocation of the original prophet, Isaiah of Jerusalem.

A final theme of Third Isaiah is the belief that God's salvation will touch all people, not just the Chosen Ones. Worship of the one true God and the Lord's salvation are a universal call and gift, meant for all people: "For my house will be called a house of prayer for all peoples" (Is 56:7).

Obadiah: Vengeance. The book of Obadiah consists of twenty-one verses, the shortest book in the Old Testament. Details about the author's life are unknown. The prophetic utterances target the Edomites, decendants of Jacob's brother, Esau, and traditional enemies of the Israelites. They had moved into southern Judah and participated in the sack of Jerusalem. In addition, they were among those who re-

■ *journal* ■

Read Zec 8:1–23. In your journal, list five things that will take place in the Messianic age.

■ *journal* ■

Read either Joel or Malachi and do the following in your journal.

1. Read the introduction to the particular book that appears in your Bible.
2. Briefly summarize what the book is about.
3. Copy at least five verses that speak a powerful message to you.

sisted the resettlement of the returning exiles. Obadiah sharply denounces the actions of this enemy, predicts their destruction, and prophesies the restoration of Judah.

Joel: Repent.   Joel was a Temple prophet who believed that a locust plague that ravished the country was a powerful sign of God's judgment on his people. His work is a call to repentance and fasting, after which he promises God will bless the nation.

> "But now — declares Yahweh —
> come back to me with all your heart,
> fasting, weeping, mourning."
> Tear your hearts and not your clothes,
> and come back to Yahweh your God,
> for he is gracious and compassionate,
> slow to anger, rich in faithful love,
> and he relents about inflicting disaster (Jl 2:12–13).

The prophet also tells of a future "Day of the Lord" when God will battle all the evil forces (the pagan nations) at the Valley of Jehoshaphat near Jerusalem. This day will mark an entirely new beginning, a fresh creation of the world when God will pour out his spirit on all humanity.

Because Joel quotes or alludes to many other Old Testament prophets, scholars believe it is one the last prophetic books composed. It was an important book for the early Christian community. Peter, for example, quotes chapter 3 of Joel on Pentecost.

journal

Compare Joel 3 to Acts 2:14–21. Note the difference in Peter's version.

Malachi.   Malachi's name means "my messenger." Though the prophet is anonymous, he gives an accurate picture of life in the Jewish community between the period of Haggai and Nehemiah and Ezra's reforms. Attached to the Temple, Malachi's predominant theme is fidelity to God's covenant and its teachings.

The Jewish priests were making a mockery of their worship of the Lord. They offered lame, blemished, blind animals instead of the clean ones required by the Law. The prophet challenged them: would they dare to give the same kind of gifts to the governor?

Malachi also denounces the people. They divorced their wives to marry wealthy Gentile women. They rationalized their immoral behavior with twisted logic, claiming that God is pleased with sinners. But God will have none of it: "Have respect for your own life then, and do not break faith with the wife of your youth. For I hate divorce, says Yahweh" (Mal 2:15–16).

Malachi also prophesies a coming messenger who will announce the Day of the Lord. On this day of judgment God will purify the priests and the Temple, save the faithful, and usher in the reign of God.

The book of Malachi is fittingly the last book in the Old Testament canon. Its concluding verses serve as a bridge between the testaments. First, they remind the Jews to be faithful to the Mosaic Law. Second, they look hopefully forward to the Day of the Lord:

> "Look, I shall send you the prophet Elijah before the great and awesome Day of Yahweh comes. He will reconcile parents to their children and children to their parents, to forestall my putting the country under the curse of destruction" (Mal 3:23–24).

∎ *focus questions* ∎

1. Discuss how the book of Jonah counteracts the tendency toward exclusivism in the post-exilic Jewish community.
2. Describe life during the Babylonian Captivity.
3. Identify Second Isaiah (Isaiah of Babylon).
4. Identify and discuss the importance of Cyrus of Persia.
5. Briefly discuss three key themes in Second Isaiah.
6. Who or what is the Suffering Servant?
7. What is the restoration? Discuss some ways Judaism was different after the restoration than before.
8. What viewpoint did the two books of Chronicles take?
9. Identify Ezra and Nehemiah and discuss their contributions to post-exilic Judaism.
10. When did Haggai prophesy? What was his major concern?
11. Discuss one way Zechariah's message differed from Haggai's.
12. What were two concerns of Third Isaiah?
13. Identify Obadiah.
14. How was Joel's message a traditional prophetic message? What is important about the third chapter of Joel?

∎ *discuss* ∎

Read Mt 17:9–13. To whom does Jesus say this passage applies?

What are signs of lackluster worship in our own church? What can be done to improve the situation?

15. Why is it appropriate that Malachi is the last book of the Old Testament canon? What are some of its concerns?

16. Identify the following:

> Zerubbabel   Joshua   Samaritans

▪ *exercises* ▪

1. Write your own version of the Jonah story to emphasize God's love for everyone.

2. Compose a short prayer to God. Address God as you would a loving mother.

▪ *vocabulary* ▪

Copy the meaning of the following words into the vocabulary section of your journal:

discern
penitential
personification

■

Prayer Reflection

Psalm 102 is a heartfelt prayer begging God for help at a time of misfortune. It may have been composed during or shortly after the Exile. It expresses sorrow, but also confident hope that God will remain true to his promises. You may want to pray this penitential psalm that combines both a personal complaint and a national prayer for restoring Jerusalem. It begins this way:

> Yahweh, hear my prayer,
> let my cry for help reach you.
> Do not turn away your face from me
> when I am in trouble;
> bend down and listen to me,
> when I call, be quick to answer me! (Ps 102:1–2).

■ *reflection* ■

Where do you most need God's help right now?

■ *resolution* ■

God uses you to help others who are also in need. Find someone who needs you and offer your service as a sign of your gratitude for the help God has given you in the past.

■

chapter 9

The Wisdom and Prayer of Israel

But you, our God, are kind and true, slow to anger, governing the universe with mercy. Even if we sin, we are yours, since we acknowledge your power, but we will not sin, knowing we count as yours. To know you is indeed the perfect virtue, and to know your power is the root of immortality.

— Wisdom 15:1–3

Perhaps you have heard of the harried college student who sent an urgent telegram to his parents: "Am without money or friends. In desperate need of help."

Not to be outdone, his father at once sent back a reply: "Make friends."

Parents like to give advice to their children. Their experience of the ways of the world has given them a perspective that can help the younger generation live a fuller, happier life. This is not to say that children like getting advice or that they will follow it.

Every culture has its collection of proverbs, wise sayings, and clever stories to help people live meaningful lives. Israel's wisdom writers borrowed from neighbors such as Egypt, Mesopotamia, Greece, and Canaan, as well as adding their own unique insights. They adapted and transformed the materials at hand to teach that Yahweh worked through human experience.

The wisdom writers studied God's creation and the laws built into it. Their observations enabled them to instruct, advise, and persuade others to live in harmony with the order God established. Using riddles, parables, metaphors, and wise sayings, they taught that living a good human life would lead to happiness and success. Most wisdom writers and teachers also strongly believed and taught the theory of retribution: the good will be rewarded, and the evil will be punished.

Israel's wisdom literature exposes us to a key insight: "The first principle of wisdom is the fear of Yahweh" (Prv 9:10). This is a healthy recognition that God is God and we are God's creatures. We must respect God's majesty and realize in true humility that the Lord is the source of our life

169

and all our gifts. Worshiping God with awe is the beginning
of true religion.

■

Sound Advice

The book of Proverbs is a textbook of right and wise
living. Its short, pithy phrases teach right and wrong. Its
wisdom stems from profound reverence for and obedience
to God. Beginning with fear of the Lord, Proverbs touches on
many themes: home, work, relationships, justice, our words,
our attitudes and decisions.

One of Proverbs' key themes is on the right use of speech.
What we say to others reveals who we are. The tongue has
power for both good and evil.

Study the following proverbs. Then read the reflection
statement that follows. Rate yourself according to the following scale: **1** — describes me well; **2** — describes me most of
the time; **3** — does not describe me.

_____ 1. Liars' lips are a cover for hatred,
whoever utters slander is a fool (Prv 10:18).
Reflection: I am a person of truth.

_____ 2. A tittle-tattler lets secrets out,
the trustworthy keeps things hidden (Prv 11:13).
Reflection: I can keep confidences.

_____ 3. The fool shows anger straightaway,
the discreet conceals dislike (Prv 12:16).
Reflection: When angry, I allow myself to cool off
before responding.

_____ 4. A guard on the mouth makes life secure,
whoever talks too much is lost (Prv 13:3).
Reflection: I speak when appropriate. I am not a
constant babbler.

_____ 5. A mild answer turns away wrath,
sharp words stir up anger (Prv 15:1).
Reflection: I can be counted on to soothe the feelings of others. My motto is that of St. Francis de
Sales: "A teaspoon of honey attracts more flies
than a barrel of vinegar."

_____ 6. To retort without listening
is both foolish and embarrassing (Prv 18:13).
Reflection: I listen carefully to others before
speaking.

_____ 7. Let someone else sing your praises, but not your
own mouth,
a stranger, but not your own lips (Prv 27:2).
Reflection: I am humble, not a bragger.

▪ *journal* ▪

A major theme of Proverbs is harmonious living in the family. Read the following selections on parents and children. Write a short reflection saying whether you agree or disagree with some of the advice given.

10:1	22:6, 15
13:1, 24	23:13–16, 19–28
17:21, 25	28:7, 24
19:3, 18, 27	29:15, 17
20:11	30:11, 17

▪ *discuss* ▪

Is spanking a child a good method of discipline? Explain.

▪ *class reading assignment* ▪

1. Read one chapter of Proverbs 10—29. More than one student can be responsible for a given chapter.
2. Copy your three favorite proverbs from the chapter you read into your journal. Write a short interpretation of the proverb.
3. Share with your classmates one or two of the proverbs you selected. Discuss your interpretation.

▪

Proverbs: Guide for Successful Living

Proverbs embodies the wisdom tradition of Israel. Wisdom is the virtue that enables one to live an upright life in God's presence.

During the reigns of David and Solomon, foreign nobles and wise men often visited the court at Jerusalem. Solomon himself had a great reputation for wisdom. Thus, the editors of Proverbs ascribe authorship to him. The book of Kings tells us he wrote three thousand proverbs (1 Kgs 5:12). Proverbs is actually the result of a complex development that began in the time of the kings, but culminated in a final editing in the late sixth or early fifth century B.C.

The heart of the book is two collections of proverbs: "the proverbs of Solomon" (10:1—22:16) containing 375 aphorisms, or sayings, and 128 aphorisms "transcribed by the men of Hezekiah" (25:1—29:27). The proverbs are excellent teaching tools. In a crisp saying they give advice, encouragement, and directions for living. They primarily teach three types of wisdom — the knowledge of God's created world, the skill of making right choices, and the art of living before God.

Proverbs' chief literary technique is the *maschal*, a Hebrew word that means comparison. Most proverbs are two-liners that use one of three forms of the device known as parallelism:

1) *Synonymous parallelism* — the second line restates the first. For example:

> Pride goes before destruction,
> a haughty spirit before a fall (Prv 16:18).

2) *Antithetical parallelism* — the second line contrasts with the first but teaches the same idea. For example:

> A wise child is a father's joy,
> a foolish child a mother's grief (Prv 10:1).

3) *Synthetic parallelism* — the second line advances the thought of the first. For example:

> White hairs are a crown of honor,
> they are found in the ways of uprightness (Prv 16:31).

Theological Themes. Proverbs stresses the creative wisdom of God; the wise person can discover God by studying the world God created, and in turn, knowledge of God will lead to knowledge of the created world. The heart of true happiness and the way to wisdom is to reverence God as the source of all wisdom and to obey the divine laws.

■ *discuss* ■

Prv 1:1—9:18 serves as a lengthy introduction to Proverbs. It treats the value of wisdom. Read *Prv 1:1–33*.

What are some values to gaining wisdom?

Ecclesiastes: All Is Vanity

The first verse of Ecclesiastes identifies its author as Qoheleth, the son of King David. Like Proverbs, Ecclesiastes is ascribed to the wisest of kings. But scholars date the book around the third century B.C., written perhaps in Phoenicia or Egypt by a philosopher influenced by Greek thought. The name Qoheleth translates the Hebrew word for *assembly* and refers to someone who presides over a meeting, a preacher or teacher.

Ecclesiastes is a loose, rambling collection of poems, proverbs, laments, and rhetorical questions. Some scholars divide the book into two parts — Qoheleth's observations on life and the conclusions he draws from those observations.

Theological Themes.   We find the central theme of the book in its second verse: "Vanity of vanities, . . . vanity of vanities! All things are vanity" (1:2, NAB). The Hebrew word we translate as *vanity* also means "breath, mist, vapor, or thin air." It refers to that which vanishes. Vanity is anything that is insubstantial and fleeting. And for Qoheleth, everything under the sun is passing.

Ecclesiastes, on first reading, appears pessimistic about life. The author has tried acquiring material possessions, pursuing sensual pleasure, seeking power and prestige — and has found only emptiness. He concludes that much of what we consider important is meaningless and leads only to death. God has given us life, so we should live it fully in the present, remembering that everything we do on earth will ultimately fade away.

But Qoheleth also trusts God. Though life to us is a mystery. God is in control and will judge humans, so we should not neglect the divine law:

> To sum up the whole matter: fear God and keep his commandments, for that is the duty of everyone. For God will call our deeds to judgment, all that is hidden, be it good or bad (Eccl 12:13–14).

--- ■ ---

Sampling Ecclesiastes

Please read Eccl 1:1—3:22 and answer the following questions:

1. What does 1:9–10 mean?

2. Read 2:18. What bothers Qoheleth?

3. Refer to 3:1–15. What positive statement about God is made here?

■ *journal* ■

Rewrite Eccl 3:1–9 from the viewpoint of a contemporary student. Or using pictures from magazines, create a booklet to illustrate these famous verses.

■ *discuss* ■

Is Qoheleth a realist, a cynic, or a skeptic? Explain each term.

--- ■ ---

Song of Songs

■ *journal* ■

Read Song of Songs 4:1–16.

What, to you, is the most appealing image of the beloved?

■ *discuss* ■

4:12 refers to the beloved as a sister (a term of endearment) and speaks of a closed garden, a symbol of virginity.

Would our contemporary society agree with the ideal stated here?

There is no other biblical book like Song of Songs (meaning the greatest of songs). Although it is ascribed to Solomon, anonymous poets composed this work during the period of restoration. It is a collection of poems that celebrate the passion, joy, and springtime freshness of the physical attraction between a man and a woman.

Song of Songs praises and celebrates God's beautiful gift of sexual love. A basic truth of this book is that God has blessed and created our sexual nature. We should joyfully accept ourselves and thank God for his goodness and wisdom in making us the way we are.

Song of Songs has lent itself to many interpretations over the years. Both Jews and Christians have seen in it an allegory, an extended comparison in which the man and woman represent a spiritual reality. Jewish commentators see in it an analogy of God's passionate love for Israel. Christians see the lovers as symbols for Christ and the church. The Lord is the bridegroom, the church is the bride. Saints Bernard of Clairvaux and John of the Cross saw these poems as a description of God's union with the soul of the individual believer.

Others interpret the Song of Songs as a liturgical drama that took place in the spring. Still others claim it is a series of songs sung during a week-long wedding feast when the bride and groom were crowned queen and king.

Perhaps, though, the literal meaning is the best. Song of Songs celebrates a wonderful gift God has given to us: the sexual expression of love. Its lesson is that this gift should not lead to promiscuity. God's design is that we should celebrate sexual love only in marriage — a permanent, faithful, and exclusive commitment between a husband and wife.

Wisdom

Wisdom was probably the last book composed in Old Testament times, perhaps around one hundred years before Christ. The anonymous author was a Jew from Alexandria in Egypt. Like the authors of other wisdom writings, he appealed to the authority of Solomon. The Greek title of the book is the Wisdom of Solomon.

The book of Wisdom is written in Greek. This made Jewish scholars in the first century omit it from the official list of books they considered inspired. The author shows a brilliant knowledge of the key events of salvation history, especially the Exodus. He lived during the time that his fellow-Jews were turning from their faith to embrace the Greek culture that had become dominant in Egypt and throughout the ancient world. He may also have been writing to Gentiles, hoping to lead them to God, whose love is open to all.

Wisdom can be divided into three sections:

1. *The Book of Eschatology ("the last things") (1:1—6:21).* A major theme of these chapters is that while human destiny is in God's hands, our choices in life make a difference. Some ideas new to Judaism emerge in these chapters. For example, Wisdom teaches that contrary to Jewish belief, childlessness is not necessarily a curse from God. Wisdom teaches that it is

journal

Read Wisdom 2:23—3:12. Answer the following questions.

1. What was God's original intent for humans?
2. Where did death enter the picture?
3. What will happen to the souls of the just?

better to be sterile than to have godless children. These chapters also tell us that suffering is not always the result of personal sin. Innocent and good people do suffer. Wisdom teaches that sometimes

> God was putting them to the test
> and has proved them worthy to be with him;
> he has tested them like gold in a furnace,
> and accepted them as a perfect burnt offering (Wis 3:5–6).

Another major idea is the introduction of the Greek concept of the immortal soul. Prior to the second century B.C. the Jews did not have a clearly expressed belief in immortality. They accepted death as a limit ordained by God. As we have seen, old age and posterity were considered a blessing. Under the influence of Greek thought, the idea of individual immortality began to take shape. The virtuous person who lives wisely is destined to live eternally with God in the afterlife.

2. *Praise of Wisdom (6:22—11:1).* These chapters encourage us to seek God's wisdom. The author personifies Wisdom, referring to it as the spirit of the Lord. He then reviews the high points of Jewish history to show how God's wisdom was present at the creation of the world, how it inspired the patriarchs, and how it guided the Israelites during the Exodus.

3. *Meditation on the Exodus (11:2—19:22).* These chapters meditate on the meaning of Exodus, focusing on two ideas: first, the sufferings of the Egyptians resulted from their sins; second, the evils that befell Israel's enemies were God's way of saving his friends. The purpose of this section was to encourage Alexandrian Jews to remain faithful to a God most worthy of their trust.

Sirach (Ecclesiasticus): Living Wisely

The longest of the wisdom books at fifty-one chapters, Sirach is the only biblical work that identifies its author: Jesus, son of Eleazor son of Sirach. This devoted grandson tells us in the foreword of the book that he has translated his grandfather's work into Greek from the Hebrew. The translation took place shortly after 132 B.C. in Egypt.

Sirach composed his collection of proverbs and reflections between 190–175 B.C., most likely in Jerusalem, to show the

Jews that true wisdom can be found in the faith of Israel and not in the pagan philosophies of Greece and other cultures.

The book of Sirach is also known as Ecclesiasticus ("The Book of the Church") because it was the most important of the writings not found in the Hebrew scriptures to be incorporated into the Vulgate (the Latin Christian Bible). It contains many maxims, grouped thematically, on topics of interest for every age: friendship, family relationships, education, economic livelihood, worship, and the like. Part 1 (Chapters 1—43) contains moral instruction; part 2 (44:1—50:24) praises the heroes of Israel's history.

Like the other wisdom writings, it teaches that wisdom comes from God and the way to wisdom is fear of the Lord. An original contribution of Sirach, however, is in joining wisdom to keeping the Law. The author also teaches careful performance of religious duties, especially proper worship.

Sampling Sirach

In Sirach, we find good practical advice on many topics. Please read the following passages. Copy into your journal a verse or two from each section that especially hit home.

Friendship: 6:5–17	*Proper use of speech*: 19:5–16
Family life: 7:18–28	*Wine-drinking*: 31:25–31
Exercise of freedom: 15:11–20	*Good advice*: 37:11–15

Women: Sirach reflects the harsh attitude toward women of a patriarchal society. It probably exemplifies this attitude more than any other Old Testament book (see, for example, Sir 25:13–26). Even when Sirach has positive things to say about a good wife, it is expressed from the husband's point of view. *Read Sir 26:1–4, 13–18*. Then discuss the following questions:

- How is our society still biased against women?
- Is the church itself guilty of sexist attitudes toward women? Explain.
- What can or should be done about your conclusions?

Job: Why Do People Suffer?

No one knows who crafted Job, a superb drama, but scholars date the work between 500–400 B.C. The story is ancient, probably predating the reign of Solomon. The old prose tale appears at the beginning (1:1—2:13) and the end of the book of Job (42:7–17). Between the tale is the poetic heart of the book. It consists of a debate between Job and his friends and God's reply.

The Story.   Everyone can relate to the story of Job. A rich oriental sheik, Job, religious and morally upright, received many blessings from God. He had many children, wealth measured in livestock, slaves to command, and the respect of others. But suddenly, for no apparent reason, tragedy strikes. He loses his possessions; his children perish; and he suffers a loathsome skin disease. Before long, Job was an outcast, waiting for death near the city dump.

Our hearts go out to Job and we ask the timeless question: "Why does a good, loving God allow innocent people to suffer?" A contemporary form of this same question is: "Why do bad things happen to good people?" The book wrestles with this profound and important question. In a cycle of speeches, friends of Job provide him with traditional answers. The cast of characters include Eliphaz, a kind mystic; Bildad, a harsh traditionalist; and Zophar, a narrow dogmatist. In one form or another, they offer variations of these two arguments:

1. "You are suffering, Job, because you sinned. God punishes sinners."
2. "God sends trials to those he loves, Job. You are suffering because God loves you."

Job, however, cannot accept either argument. Why would God treat his friends this way? To the end he protests his innocence:

> Far from admitting you to be in the right,
> I shall maintain my integrity to my dying day.
> I take my stand on my uprightness, I shall not stir:
> in my heart I need not be ashamed of my days (Job 27:5–6).

Shortly after the speeches of Job's friends, a much younger friend of Job — Elihu the Buzite — enters the picture. He has listened carefully to the arguments and has reached a different conclusion than the others. Elihu claims that pride taints Job and is somehow adding to his punishment. Job has had only one wish all along: to see God and not merely hear from his friends what God is thinking. Job believes that if

God would draw near to him, God would see Job's goodness and justify him.

Eventually, God does draw near to Job. In 38:1—42:6, God answers Job, but God's answers go far beyond the questions. God does not settle the question of innocent suffering. Rather, God asks Job:

> Where were you when I laid the earth's foundations?
> Tell me, since you are so well-informed! (Job 38:4).

Who is Job, a mere creature, to question almighty God? God is a mystery. God's ways are beyond human comprehension. God wants personal faith and trust, belief, not full understanding, as Job wanted or his friends pridefully pretended to have.

Job repents. The book ends on a happy note. God fully restores Job and once again Job prospers. Job's words to God echo down the centuries. They reveal a model for everyone who demands an answer from God:

> I was the man who misrepresented your intentions
>   with my ignorant words.
> You have told me about great works that I cannot
>   understand,
>   about marvels which are beyond me, of which I
>   know nothing.
> Before, I knew you only by hearsay
>   but now, having seen you with my own eyes,
> I retract what I have said,
>   and repent in dust and ashes (Job 42:3, 5–6).

Christians believe Job's question receives a powerful answer on the cross of Jesus Christ. Jesus is the only true innocent. Yet, he suffered the burden of human sin so all of humanity can gain eternal life. Suffering joined to the cross of Jesus has redemptive value in God's mysterious plan of salvation.

Sampling Job

Read the following chapters of Job and answer the questions in your journal.

1. Job 1—2.

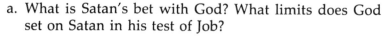

■ *reflection* ■

Describe a time when you grew through suffering.

■ *discuss* ■

Who are the innocents who suffer today?

a. What is Satan's bet with God? What limits does God set on Satan in his test of Job?

b. Quote a verse that proves Job's steadfast faith in God.

2. Read Job 4—5 as a sample of the line of argument used to explain Job's sufferings.

a. How does Eliphaz explain Job's suffering?

b. What does he want Job to do?

3. Job 31. How does Job defend himself?

4. Job 38. What is the Lord driving at?

Psalms

The Psalms express the gamut of human emotion and experience — joy, grief, devotion, sorrow, prayer, lament, consolation, community celebration, depression, faith, thanksgiving. Although the 150 psalms grew out of an individual's or Israel's own experience, they express timeless themes.

The Psalms are the hymn book of ancient Israel. A good way to think of them is to remember that they are poems that were meant to be sung. Most of these prayer-poems were composed as part of the liturgical worship in the Temple. Many of their titles contain instructions for the choirmaster. For example, psalms 4 and 6 instruct: "For the leader; with stringed instruments" (v.1, NAB).

Who Wrote the Psalms?   The Psalter (another name for the book of Psalms) spans close to a thousand years of literary activity. Many anonymous poets were responsible for them. The inscriptions attribute seventy-three of them to David, but the phrase "of David" probably also means "for" or "about" David or another king in David's lineage. Tradition held that David was responsible for introducing music into the sanctuary. Thus, the Israelites ascribed the psalms/songs to David in the same way they assigned proverbs to Solomon.

David, a gifted poet and musician, undoubtedly composed some of them and probably collected others. The opening verse of some psalms identify other authors who may have been poets attached to the Temple or cantors who led the communal singing.

Division of the Psalter. There are five major divisions in the Psalter, perhaps corresponding to the five books of the Pentateuch. Psalm 1 serves as an introduction to the book of Psalms. At the end of the last psalm in each of the first four books of the Psalter is a *doxology*, a prayer praising God, to mark the end of that particular book. Psalm 150 is a short doxology that concludes the entire collection. It is a rousing call to "Let everything that breathes praise Yahweh. Alleluia!" (Ps 150:6).

Types of Psalms. Many have tried to classify and organize the psalms, for example, thematically. A common classification, though, is by *literary type*, used, for example, in the *New Jerusalem Bible*. These types are listed below.

1. *Hymns.* These psalms praise God and God's works. They include *enthronement hymns* that celebrate God's kingship and *songs of Zion* which show devotion to the holy city of Jerusalem. These psalms typically have the following organizational pattern:

   a. an invitation to praise God;
   b. the body of the psalm, which gives the reasons for praising God;
   c. the conclusion which either repeats the introduction or expresses a prayer.

2. *Supplications.* These psalms address God directly. They make up the largest category of psalms. They include both *individual* and *community laments*. Individuals ask for freedom from sickness or false accusations and the nation begs deliverance in time of crisis or suffering. The structure of the lament includes:

   a. calling on God's name;
   b. description of the need;
   c. petition for deliverance;
   d. motivation for granting the deliverance;
   e. expression of confidence in God.

3. *Thanksgiving.* Gratitude to God is the major theme of psalms of thanksgiving. These psalms include both communal and individual thanksgivings. Their structure is similar to that of the hymns.

4. *Others.* Included in this category are psalms that express an individual song of confidence (Ps 23), prophetic oracles delivered during the Temple ceremonies (Ps 75), and reflections on problems of human living addressed by other wisdom literature (Ps 1, 49, 53, 73).

The five major divisions in the book of Psalms are:

   Book 1: Ps 1—41
   Book 2: Ps 42—72
   Book 3: Ps 73—89
   Book 4: Ps 90—106
   Book 5: Ps 107—150

Certain psalms speak to Christians because they sing of a coming Messiah, an anointed one of Yahweh. This is especially true of Psalms 2, 72, and 110, the most frequently quoted psalms in the New Testament. Certain other psalms, for example, the enthronement hymns and psalms that talk about kingship also find their fulfillment in the New Testament. And Psalm 23, which speaks of God as the shepherd who watches out for his flock, calls to mind Jesus, the Good Shepherd.

▪ *assignment* ▪

Hymns:

1. Read Ps 33 and Ps 104. Note in your journal how the psalmist describes God's wondrous creation.
2. Read Ps 93. Note in your journal the description of God's kingship.
3. Read Ps 103. List some attributes of God.
4. Read Ps 100, Ps 136, and Ps 146. As you read these psalms, mark in your Bibles the three sections of the hymn as outlined above.

Supplications:

5. Read Ps 22. Note in your journal several passages that apply to Jesus.
6. Read Ps 38. Mark in your Bible the various sections of the psalm as outlined above.
7. Read Ps 51. What is the psalmist's understanding of sin (verse 4)?

Thanksgiving:

8. Read Ps 118. For what is the psalmist grateful?

Others:

9. Read Ps 1. What are the two ways?
10. Read Ps 89. What covenant is being described in verses 19–37?
11. Read Psalms 2, 72, and 110. Note in your journal at least five verses that point to Jesus the Christ.

Message of the Psalms.   Since the psalms are prayers addressed to God, they touch on many theological themes that were at the heart of Israel's story. For example, the psalms recognize the sovereignty of God and praise the Lord for his power and creative activity. The Lord's good creation and the gift of life reveal his glory; they bring us untold joy.

The psalms also proclaim God as the savior of the people, both the individual and the nation. Though God can never be fully known, the Lord has proven trustworthy, true to the divine promises and the covenant.

Many of the psalms view human beings as helpless, suffering, guilty of sin, and in need of God's unending mercy and compassion. They teach that the Lord is a just God. In the end, the Lord will right all wrongs. Because of God's justice and goodness, we should be humble, thankful, repentant, full of faith, and prayerful. God deserves our unending praise!

▪ *focus questions* ▪

1. What is the theory of retribution?

2. Explain how the "fear of the Lord" is the beginning of wisdom.

3. According to the wisdom books, what is the value of the virtue of wisdom?

4. What is a *maschal*? Why is the proverb a good teaching device?

5. Complete the following chart:

Book	Date	A key theological point
Proverbs	_____	_____
Ecclesiastes	_____	_____
Song of Songs	_____	_____
Wisdom	_____	_____
Sirach	_____	_____
Job	_____	_____

6. Explain and give an example of these forms of parallelism in the book of Proverbs: synonymous, antithetical, synthetic.

7. Identify *Qoheleth*. What did he mean by "everything is vanity"?

8. Discuss two possible interpretations of the meaning of Song of Songs.

9. What new theological ideas about suffering and eternal destiny does the book of Wisdom introduce?

10. What is unique about the book of Sirach?

11. What age-old problem does the book of Job treat?

12. What are some traditional answers to the reasons for Job's sufferings?

13. How does God "answer" Job?

14. What form of literature are the psalms?

15. To whom are about half of the psalms ascribed? Why?

16. How many major divisions are there in the Psalter? Why?

17. Briefly explain three major types of psalms from a *literary* point of view.

■ *vocabulary* ■

Copy the meaning of these words into the vocabulary section of your journal.

antithetical
aphorism
retribution

--- ■ ---

Prayer Reflection

The most beloved of all psalms is Psalm 23. Slowly and prayerfully read it aloud.

> The Lord is my shepherd, I shall lack nothing.
>   He makes me lie down in green pastures,
> he leads me beside quiet waters,
>   he restores my soul.
> He guides me in paths of righteousness
>   for his name's sake.
> Even though I walk
>   through the valley of the shadow of death,
> I will fear no evil,
>   for you are with me;
> your rod and your staff,
>   they comfort me.
> You prepare a table before me
>   in the presence of my enemies.
> You anoint my head with oil;
>   my cup overflows.
> Surely goodness and love will follow me
>   all the days of my life,
> and I will dwell in the house of the Lord
>   forever.

(New International Version)

▪ *reflection* ▪

The psalmist recalls God's loving protection by reflecting on the image of God as shepherd, one who looks out for his flock. The psalmist focuses on the divine shepherd's constant care of the sheep, the peace he brings, and the shepherd's healing powers. The psalmist also knows that the Lord will protect us from danger — sickness, violence, accidents, and other harm.

Psalm 23 also stresses the image of the divine host, one who will celebrate a festive meal with his guests. Drawing on the Eastern practice of hospitality shown to the traveler, the psalmist knows the Lord will protect us from enemies, will refresh us from the weariness of life, and will welcome us with joy and gladness. God will also keep the terms of the covenant.

Christians see in this beautiful psalm a foreshadowing of Jesus who knows and saves his sheep and who will lead them to a heavenly banquet in eternity.

▪ *resolution* ▪

Rewrite this psalm in terms that appeal to you. Pick two images of God that speak to your heart. What has God done for you in the past? What will he do for you in the future? Write your version of Psalm 23 in poetic form.

chapter 10

Hope Amidst Change

The Last Books of the Old Testament

I was gazing into the visions of the night,
when I saw, coming on the clouds of heaven,
as it were a son of man....
On him was conferred rule,
honor and kingship,
and all peoples, nations and languages became his
   servants.
His rule is an everlasting rule
which will never pass away,
and his kingship will never come to an end.
                    — Daniel 7:13–14

A six-year old child was going through a children's Bible. She was circling the word *God* whenever she found it on a page. Her mother, startled, asked, "Why are you doing that to your new book?"

The child answered innocently, "Because now I'll know where to find God when I need him."

As we near the end of our study of the Old Testament, this story can remind us that God's word is always near us. A famous Protestant preacher said it well years ago: "A Bible which is falling apart usually belongs to someone who isn't." How well-used is your Bible? Do you look for God in it? What does God's word say to you?

In this chapter we will sample three short stories the Jews told to bolster faith, to edify, and to teach a religious or moral message. We will then look to the story of the Jews from the time of their return to the Promised Land down to New Testament times. Our Christian faith owes much to the Jewish faith that developed during this era.

■

Old Testament Faith and You

As we conclude our study of the Hebrew scriptures, let us list several beliefs about God and reality that appear throughout the Old Testament. Evaluate your level of belief in these statements by circling the proper number. **5** represents strong belief; **1** means you are struggling with this.

1. **There is only one God.** God alone is holy. God is the creator, ruler, and provider. God alone deserves our highest worship.   1 2 3 4 5

2. **God cares about us.** God is actively involved in the world, saving and redeeming it. God is also active in my life.   1 2 3 4 5

3. **God invites us to return his friendship.** We do this by praising the Lord, praying, and obeying the divine law.   1 2 3 4 5

4. **A key way to love God is by loving our neighbor.**   1 2 3 4 5

5. **To follow the Lord of the Hebrew scriptures, we must passionately commit ourselves to justice.** This means we must help the poor and suffering in our midst.   1 2 3 4 5

6. **We must be a people of hope.** God's world is essentially good. There is much to look forward to, especially the coming reign of God.   1 2 3 4 5

7. **The beginning of wisdom is the fear of the Lord.** We should be humble before the Lord, recognizing that God is the source of all our gifts. God is a mystery we can never control. Are we under God's authority? Does God rule our lives?   1 2 3 4 5

. journal .

Write a brief essay explaining which belief from the Hebrew scriptures speaks most forcefully to you. Explain why.

. discuss .

Give several concrete examples of how young people living in today's complex world can put statements 3–7 into practice, making them *living* faith statements.

Stories With a Message

These three stories come from the time after the Exile. Each inspires people to remain faithful and brave during troublesome times.

Tobit.   The book of Tobit, written by an unknown author around 200 B.C., praises the virtuous Jew and speaks of God's mercy and benevolence. This entertaining story teaches many lessons. For example, it praises traditional forms of Jewish piety — prayer, fasting, and almsgiving. It lauds family life and stresses fidelity to the community in activities such as burying the dead, honoring one's parents, caring for the poor. Finally, it teaches that God will never abandon us if we remain faithful. Even in trying times of personal or national troubles, God will remember us and answer our prayers.

Although Tobit comes after 1–2 Chronicles and Ezra-Nehemiah, the book is not a true historical book. The author draws some historical details from the past to tell a fictional story. The book of Tobit shares many themes with the wisdom writings.

The story highlights three people: Tobit, his son Tobias, and Tobit's relative Sarah. Tobit was an exile in ancient Nineveh sometime after the fall of the northern kingdom. He kept the Law and dispensed charity. He also helped those in need, despite personal risk. For example, he buried the dead though forbidden to do so by his Assyrian overlords. One night, exhausted from this act of charity, he fell asleep in his garden and bird droppings falling in his eyes blinded him. Depressed, he begged God to let him die.

His kinsman's daughter, Sarah, was equally depressed. An evil demon, who lusted after Sarah, jealously killed seven of Sarah's husbands on their wedding night. She, too, prayed for death. God hears the prayers of both Tobit and Sarah and responds to them in a surprising and merciful way. Despite their misfortunes, God is in control of their destinies and will bring good out of their tragic situations.

The Lord sends the archangel Raphael disguised as a young man. The angel accompanies Tobit's son, Tobias, to Media to claim some money and to take Sarah as his wife. On the way, a large fish attacks Tobias, but Raphael orders him to kill it and to remove its gall, heart, and liver. They will make useful medicines. At their destination, Raphael instructs Tobias to marry Sarah, a woman with whom Tobias fell madly in love. Raphael also orders Tobias to burn the fish's heart and liver in the bridal chamber to drive out the evil demon.

With the money he had gone to claim and many expensive gifts from a very generous father-in-law, Tobias returns to his anxious parents. He rubs the fish's gall into his father's eyes, a remedy that cures Tobit of his blindness. This happy ending calls forth from Tobit a beautiful hymn of praise to God.

Finally, before revealing his identity to Tobit and Tobias, the angel Raphael teaches them some important lessons:

> "Bless God, utter his praise before all the living.... Bless and extol his name. Proclaim before all people the deeds of God as they deserve, and never tire of giving him thanks.... Prayer with fasting and alms with uprightness are better than riches with iniquity. Better to practice almsgiving than to hoard up gold" (Tb 12:6, 8).

The lessons in the Book of Tobit are uplifting and challenge us to live our lives for others.

Judith. Written around the beginning of the first century B.C., the book of Judith is a fictional work that teaches a familiar lesson: God cares deeply for a faithful Israel. The many anachronisms and factual errors tell us the story is not historical. For example, it says Nebuchadnezzar is king of Assyria when in fact, he was king of Babylon.

The heroine of the story — Judith — is also not a historical person. The name Judith simply means "Jewish woman." The Judith of this story embodies notable Israelite women who saved Israel in the past — Miriam, who led the people in thanksgiving after the Exodus; Deborah, who bolstered the people's faith when they were under attack; and Jael, who assassinated an enemy leader.

Part 1 of the story (Jdt 1—7) tells how Nebuchadnezzar wanted help from western nations in a war he was waging. Israel and other nations refused to help. Furious, Nebuchadnezzar sends Holofernes, his able general, on a destructive campaign against the nations that rebuffed his request. The Jewish leaders in Jerusalem prepare for an assault by fortifying the border districts, especially the town of Bethulia which guards the strategic mountain passes.

A leading Ammonite — Achior — warns Holofernes not to attack Israel until the people sin because Yahweh always protects a faithful Israel. This advice infuriates Holofernes who binds Achior and sends him off to Bethulia where he reports to the Jewish population. Meanwhile, Holofernes cuts off the water supply to Bethulia; soon the people begin to perish and beg their leaders to surrender. The town leader, Uzziah, calls the people to vigorous prayer for another five days. If God will not answer their pleas, they will give up.

Now enters the widow Judith (Jdt 8—16) whose courage, faith, intelligence, and deep love for her people outshine the timid and despairing male Jewish leaders.

> Now she was very beautiful, charming to see. Her husband Manasseh had left her gold and silver, menservants and maidservants, herds and land; and she lived among all her possessions without anyone finding a word to say against her, so devoutly did she fear God (Jdt 8:7–8).

With God's help, she concocts a bold and brilliant plan of her own. Unarmed, she goes to the enemy camp with only one servant and deceives the Assyrians into thinking that she is betraying her own people. Her astounding beauty impresses her enemies who fall victim to her charms. When Holofernes meets her, he falls in love with her. Judith receives permission from him to eat only the blessed (*kosher*) food she has brought with her. The general also allows her to pray to God each night outside her tent under the starlit skies.

For three nights she follows her routine of praying to God. On the fourth, Holofernes invites Judith to a banquet, fully intending to seduce her. Unfortunately for him, he gets drunk and passes out. When Judith is alone with Holofernes in his tent, she takes his sword and decapitates him. She places his head in a sack and with her maid "goes off to pray." In reality, she flees to Bethulia where her message brings joy to the desperate Jews.

> "Praise God! Praise him! Praise the God who has not withdrawn his mercy from the House of Israel, but has shattered our enemies by my hand tonight!" (Jdt 13:14).

The town leaders hang Holofernes' head from the city wall and feign an attack on the Assyrians. When the enemy discovers what happened, the soldiers panic and flee in all directions. Many die at the hands of the pursuing Israelites.

What is the point of this far-fetched story? Read during the Passover celebration, the book of Judith reminds the Chosen People of how God intervenes on their behalf.

Judith represents the small, defenseless Jewish nation which the Lord has so often saved. She also stands for all the heroic Jewish women who served as God's instruments of salvation. Finally, Judith is a model Jewish woman who cherishes her faith and courageously protects her family from influences that might try to destroy it.

The church's liturgy applies to Mary, our Blessed Mother, the hymn praising Judith:

■ *reading* ■

1. Read either Tobit or Judith in its entirety.
2. In your journal, write a two or three sentence summary of the content of each chapter.
3. Select a favorite quote or passage from the work and transcribe it in your journal.

You are the glory of Jerusalem!
You are the great pride of Israel!
You are the highest honor of our race! (Jdt 15:9).

Esther.   Written perhaps at the close of the fourth century B.C., when the Persian Empire was dying, the book of Esther tells the story of the fate of some Jews in the Diaspora. Listed with the historical books, Esther is more accurately a short novel.

The story involves a powerful advisor to the Persian King Xerxes (Ahasuerus), Haman the Agagite, who wanted to kill on a single day all the Jews living in the Empire. His desire to obliterate the Jews rose out of his hatred of Mordecai, a Jewish servant of the king, who refused to kneel before Haman. Mordecai's religious faith taught him that only Yahweh deserves such worship.

Mordecai's niece, Esther, however, had become the new queen after the old queen disobeyed her husband. The former queen had refused to "show her beauty" in front of her husband and his guests while they partied in a drunken state. Esther was chosen over many others because of her outstanding beauty.

Esther became a heroine to the Jewish people because she intervened on their behalf by persuading Xerxes to reverse the decree against the Jews.

The book of Esther exists in two versions, a shorter version in Hebrew and a longer one in Greek. The Hebrew version focuses only on the human participants in the story, while the Greek text spells out God's role in saving the people. The key theological theme of Esther is God's providential protection of the Chosen People. The book also instructs the people to celebrate God's deliverance in a feast known as Purim. The feast gets its name from the Hebrew word *purim* which means "lots," referring to the lot that Haman drew to determine the day to slaughter the Jews. The Jewish people read Esther each year on the feast of Purim, celebrated in February or March.

Jewish History From Persia to Rome

When we last looked at the story of God's people, they had returned from captivity in Babylon and re-established the faith in Judea. The early returning exiles reconstructed

■ *journal* ■

Read Esther 9:20–32. Answer the following questions.

1. When should the Jews celebrate the feast of Purim?
2. How should they celebrate this feast?

the Temple. Nehemiah directed the rebuilding of Jerusalem's walls. Finally, Ezra introduced his reforms, renewing the Mosaic covenant and revitalizing the Jewish faith (around 398 B.C.). Meanwhile, other Jews remained in the Diaspora, with notable Jewish settlements in Babylon itself and Egypt.

Under the Persians.   From the time of Cyrus the Great in 538 B.C. until the rise of Alexander the Great, who toppled the Persian Empire beginning in 334 B.C. and ushered in Greek culture, Palestine was part of a large Persian province known as "Beyond the River." The Jews and other subservient nations, although lacking political independence, did have considerable religious and personal freedom under the Persians.

The official Persian religion — Zoroastrianism — became the state religion, but the Jews did not have to practice it. However, the Persian religion did influence Judaism. For example, we can see Judaism gradually adopting belief in angels. Jewish writers also assigned a larger role to fallen angels (demons) headed by Satan who opposed God. In addition, Judaism accepted another Persian belief — the resurrection of the dead. A related belief was divine punishment or reward for an evil or good life. By the second century B.C., both the book of Daniel and 2 Maccabees firmly state these beliefs.

Enter Alexander.   Alexander the Great's career was like a shooting star — brief, yet brilliant. Beginning in 336 B.C., he conquered massive territories — the Persian Empire, Egypt, and the entire Middle East. He even pushed the frontiers of his empire into India. Along the way, he established a cultural union of East and West known as Hellenism. Alexander's ideal was that all his conquered peoples should be one, with classical Greek culture serving as the unifying force. Alexander introduced common (*koine*) Greek as the official language of the Near East. It remained the predominant language for eight centuries, until about A.D. 500 when Latin supplanted it. The *Septuagint* is a *koine* Greek translation of the Hebrew scriptures which took place around 275 B.C. in Alexandria. The entire New Testament is in this language.

The Ptolemies: 323–198 B.C.   When Alexander died in 323 B.C. at the young age of 33, his four generals divided his empire. The Seleucid family took Syria, while the Ptolemies

reigned in Egypt. Both of these dynasties claimed and fought over Palestine, but the Ptolemies ruled it from 323–198 B.C.

The Ptolemies were benevolent rulers who made no concerted effort to impose Hellenistic culture on their subjects. Jews enjoyed considerable autonomy under them. For example, the Jewish community in Alexandria grew rapidly. It developed a form of Judaism that was compatible with Greek thought. Alexandrine Jews remained loyal to the Law and the Jerusalem Temple. However, they often changed their Jewish names to Greek ones and adopted Greek forms of government. They also studied Greek philosophy and increasingly used Greek food, clothing, furniture, and the like. The book of Wisdom, written in Greek at Alexandria around 100 B.C., borrowed freely from Greek philosophy.

In Israel, the Jewish people divided into two factions. Some adopted Greek customs — games, plays, athletics, education, and philosophy. Other Jews, however, deplored any assimilation of Greek culture. For them, to abandon tradition and Jewish customs was to desert the faith of the ancestors.

The Seleucids: 198–63 B.C.   In 198 B.C., the Seleucids from Syria successfully drove out the Egyptian Ptolemies and came into power in Palestine. Matters radically changed for the Jews as the Seleucid dynasty tried to impose unity on its subjects. One Seleucid ruler in particular — Antiochus IV — embodied the changed attitude. Ruling from 175–164 B.C., he arrogantly took the name *Epiphanes*, which means "god made manifest." He was intent on two goals: building a mighty army and forcing Hellenization on the colonies. This led to disaster for Jews in Israel.

To pay for his military campaigns against the Ptolemies, he twice robbed the Temple of its wealth. He erected a fort called the Citadel in the city and posted troops there to help quell rebellions and enforce his decrees. In addition, he forbade Jews to engage in practices at the very heart of their religion: circumcision, Sabbath observances, Temple sacrifices, and abstinence from pork. Worst of all, he desecrated the Temple itself in 167 B.C. by installing a statue of Zeus on the altar of holocausts. The Jews called this crime "the abomination of desolation."

Epiphanes forced Jews to choose: either abandon their faith or die a martyr's death. Many gave up their faith, sometimes at the urging of the aristocracy and corrupt high priests who favored Hellenization. But many brave and loyal Jews chose to remain faithful to Yahweh, even paying the price of torture and death.

Eventually, Antiochus IV's cruelties met vigorous resistance. When he sent an emissary to a small town near Jerusalem to enforce pagan sacrifices, the local priest, Mattathias, fought back. Although an old man, he fomented a revolt. He and his five sons took to the hills and mobilized other Jews in hiding to take up arms against the oppressors. Mattathias died shortly afterward of old age, but he appointed one son, Simeon (Simon in Greek), head of the family and another, Judas, general of the army.

1 Maccabees (c. 100 B.C.). Judas was a remarkable leader. His surname *Maccabaeus* ("hammer") identified the members of his family. The story of Judas and his brothers appears in two deuterocanonical books, 1 and 2 Maccabees.

Written in Hebrew by an anonymous author in 100 B.C., 1 Maccabees survives only in Greek translation. Chapter 1 of 1 Maccabees describes the Hellenization process that had taken place in Palestine and the atrocities of Antiochus IV. Chapter 2 reports Mattathias' revolt, while chapters 3—9 relate the career of Judas. The crowning achievement of this inspired leader's reign was the recapturing of Jerusalem, and the purification and rededication of the Temple in 164 B.C. This took place three years to the day after the "abomination of desolation." The ceremony of dedication is a high point in Jewish history, a feast commemorated each December in the Feast of Hanukkah, the festival of lights.

Judas' military exploits extended Jewish territory to Galilee in the north and to the Negev Desert in the south. After Judas fell in battle in 160 B.C., his brother Jonathan led the Jews for seventeen years (1 Mc 10—12). Jonathan won privileges from the rulers in Syria and Egypt and gained for himself the title "high priest." In 143, he fell victim to a Syrian plot, but his brother Simon took over as a most capable leader. Simon solidified the gains of his brothers and won the guarantee of Jewish independence from both Sparta and Rome (1 Mc 13—16). Simon's treacherous son-in-law killed him in 134 B.C. However, 1 Maccabees ends on a positive note: Simon's son, John Hyrcanus, becomes *ethnarch*, ruler of the people, and fills the office of high priest.

■ *research* ■

Check a dictionary of the Bible or a reference on Judaism. Prepare a short report on how our Jewish brothers and sisters celebrate the feast of Hanukkah today.

Ruins of Roman aqueduct in Caesarea

The Hasmoneans. John Hyrcanus was the first ruler in a Jewish dynasty known as the *Hasmoneans*, named after old Mattathias' father. The Hasmonean dynasty governed Judea from the Maccabean wars to the conquest by the Romans under the general Pompey (in 63 B.C.). This dynasty succeeded in bringing considerable glory and political freedom to the Jews. They extended the nation's borders to Transjordan in the east, Idumea in the south, and Galilee in the north. They took Samaria and destroyed the Samaritan temple on Mount Gerizim. They converted many pagans in these territories and founded Jewish communities.

Unfortunately, the Hasmoneans quarrelled among themselves incessantly. They went to war, forced pagans to convert, sought their own economic gain, and even crucified faithful Jews who tried to reform the corrupt regime. Eventually, the major power on the scene — Rome — stepped into the vacuum. Pompey conquered Palestine in 63 B.C., deposed the Hasmonean dynasty, and stripped the nation of many of its territorial gains. He also appointed his own high priest and set up a puppet king who ruled at the pleasure of the Roman authorities. Thus, the Jewish nation came under the thumb of Rome, which ruled until the seventh century A.D. when the Moslems began their invasions.

Herod the Great: 37–4 B.C. During the decline of the Hasmonean dynasty an Idumean, Antipater, served as minister. In 37 B.C., Antipater's son Herod became king of Judea, aided by his Roman friend Octavius, who became Emperor Augustus.

Herod was a bloodthirsty but brilliant ruler. Among his accomplishments were his building projects, most notably the port city of Caesarea on the Mediterranean Sea and the fortress Masada on the Dead Sea. Most important to the Jews, though, was Herod's magnificent rebuilding of the Jerusalem Temple. This project began in 19 B.C. but was not finished until A.D. 64, only six years before Rome levelled it during the First Jewish Revolt.

Masada, Herod's mountain fortress near the Dead Sea

Although one of Herod's ten wives was a Hasmonean, neither he nor his wife's dynasty belonged to David's family. It was during Herod's reign that a humble descendant of David, Joseph the carpenter, took his young wife to Bethlehem for a census. There, sometime between 7–4 B.C., the "King of the Jews" was born and a new era in human history began.

■

Sampling 1 Maccabees

Please read the following passages and answer the questions given.

1 Mc 1:1–62:

a. What does the author of 1 Maccabees think of Jewish Hellenizers (vv. 11–14)?

b. What were some of Antiochus' atrocities?

1 Mc 2:1–70:

a. What triggers the revolt by Mattathias?

b. Who were the *Hasideans* (v. 42)?

1 Mc 3:1—4:61:

a. Describe Judas as a leader. What were some of his accomplishments?

b. Why is Hanukkah sometimes called the "Festival of Lights" (4:50)? What else took place on this Feast of Dedication?

1 Mc 6:1–63:

a. Where and when did Antiochus IV die?

b. What heroic deed does Eleazor perform?

c. What concessions does Judas Maccabaeus win for his people?

■

2 Maccabees.   2 Maccabees is *not* a continuation of 1 Maccabees. Rather, it is an independent work by an author who condensed a much longer, five-volume work written by a certain Jason of Cyrene. Composed in Greek, perhaps around 125 B.C., 2 Maccabees reflects the spirituality of a new Jewish sect, the Pharisees.

The book covers the period from around 180–160 B.C., concluding before Judas Maccabaeus' death. The first part of the book (2 Mc 1:1—2:18) includes two letters to Egyptian Jews to gain their sympathy for what is happening in Palestine. These letters give instructions on the feasts of Booths and Hanukkah. The second part (2 Mc 2:19—10:9) summarizes Jason's account of events up to the feast of the dedication of the Temple (164 B.C.). Finally, the third section (2 Mc 10:10—15:39) treats Judas' victories up to his defeat of the Syrian general Nicanor (161 B.C.).

Theological Themes.   2 Maccabees is important for several teachings that have influenced Christian thinking and belief:

■   *Suffering can have a positive value.*   2 Maccabees relates two rousing and inspiring accounts of the martyrdoms of old Eleazor (6:18–31) and seven brothers who refused to engage in pagan practices, which led to their martyrdom. 2 Maccabees tells us:

> But the mother was especially admirable and worthy of honorable remembrance, for she watched the death of seven sons in the course of a single day, and bravely endured it because of her hopes in the Lord (2 Mc 7:20).

This suffering mother exemplified the Jewish resolve to remain steadfast. The valiant witness of the few can help reform people and bring them back to a God who will always stay by them.

■   *Resurrection of the dead.*   2 Maccabees clearly proclaims a belief in the resurrection. God will deliver the faithful who suffer at the hands of the unfaithful. Before dying, one of the courageous brothers declares:

> "Cruel brute, you may discharge us from this present life, but the King of the world will raise us up, since we die for his laws, to live again for ever" (2 Mc 7:9).

■   *Prayer for the dead has value.*   2 Mc 12:38–45 has influenced Catholic belief in the doctrine of purgatory. We should pray that God will pardon the sins of the dead and keep them from everlasting ruin.

■ *discuss* ■

Read 2 Mc 6:12—7:42.

What is the purpose of God's punishment?

1. Is a martyr a hero or a fool? Explain.
2. Is there anything you would die for? Explain.

For had he [Judas] not expected the fallen to rise again, it would have been superfluous and foolish to pray for the dead, whereas if he had in view the splendid recompense reserved for those who make a pious end, the thought was holy and devout. Hence, he had this expiatory sacrifice offered for the dead, so that they might be released from their sin (2 Mc 12:44–45).

Catholics also note 2 Mc 15:11–16 in which Judas Maccabaeus dreams that he sees the prophet Jeremiah praying for the holy city and its inhabitants. This text reinforces our belief in the *communion of saints*, the doctrine of our unity with believers in this life and the next. The holy ones who have died before us intercede in heaven on our behalf.

■ *Creation from nothing.* Finally, 2 Maccabees advances the doctrine of creation. While Genesis taught that God created by separating the elements from a primordial chaos, 2 Mc 7:28 clearly teaches that God creates from nothing (*ex nihilo*).

■ *discuss* ■

Do you have a favorite saint to whom you pray for special help when you need it? Do you pray for departed relatives? Do you ask them for help? Explain and discuss.

Daniel

The book of Daniel is an interesting but difficult Old Testament book. Jews list it with the Writings, books that include the wisdom literature and the Psalms. Our Bible includes it with the Prophets because of its many dreams and visions. But Daniel is not a typical prophetic work. It is special for the two literary forms it contains: *pious histories* meant to inspire God's people and *apocalypse*, a highly symbolic form of writing whose purpose is to encourage people in dangerous and difficult times.

Outline of Daniel. Daniel has three main divisions. Part 1 (Dn 1—6) includes six tales about a young Jew named Daniel. Along with his friends, Daniel remains faithful to God under the reigns of King Nebuchadnezzar II and the Persian kings. These tales probably originated in the Persian era (529–333 B.C.), but the anonymous author of Daniel retold them from the perspective of the persecution of the Jews by Antiochus IV.

In this first section, the Babylonian king elevates the captured exile Daniel to a position of influence at his court. There Daniel and his three companions carefully keep Jewish laws and customs, despite opposition from their jealous

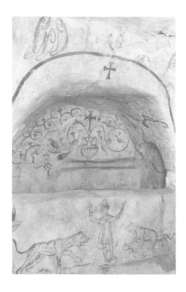

opponents at court. For example, Daniel obeys Jewish dietary laws (Dn 1) and refuses to worship pagan idols (Dn 6). For this second offense, Daniel is thrown into the lions' den, which he survives with God's intervention. His accusers, on the other hand, meet the fate they had hoped would befall Daniel. The Daniel of these chapters interprets dreams and predicts the destruction of Babylon.

The message of these inspirational stories is similar to Tobit, Judith, and Esther: God protects and blesses those who remain faithful.

Sampling Daniel

Read Daniel 1.

1. List some personal traits of the legendary hero, Daniel, and his companions:

2. On what diet did Daniel and his companions subsist? What was its result?

Read Daniel 6.

3. Why were accusations made against Daniel?

4. Why was Daniel cast in the lions' den?

5. What reversal of fortune took place?

Part 2 (Dn 7—12) contains four highly symbolic visions. They all center on the heavenly destruction of Israel's tormentors, especially Antiochus IV who was killing Jews who refused to adopt the pagan customs.

Read Dn 13. How does Daniel trap the two lecherous old men?

Part 3 (Dn 13—14) includes three other stories found only in the Septuagint (and therefore not considered inspired by Jews and Protestants). One of the stories shows a wise Daniel saving a young maiden named Susanna. He traps two elders of the community who fabricated a story that Susanna had illicit relations with a young man after she rebuffed their lustful advances.

Apocalypse (read Dn 7—12).   The middle section of Daniel (7—12), which relates the four symbolic visions, was written by an anonymous author around 164 B.C. Although this material was written at the height of Antiochus IV's persecution of the Jews, the perspective is four centuries earlier — the time of Exile.

The author chose this viewpoint for two reasons. First, he could take the role of prophet and "foretell" the future, thus proving that God is in control of events. This encouraged his persecuted sisters and brothers. The Lord will win a battle over the forces of evil, represented by Antiochus IV, and will bring peace at the end of time, the so-called "Day of the Lord."

Second, by writing about present events using symbols and past history, he could disguise his real message from the authorities and avoid persecution. The good news hidden behind the veil of symbolic language is that God would certainly defeat Antiochus IV.

Daniel 7—12 is a good example of apocalyptic writing. The Greek word for *apocalypse* translates into Latin as *revelare* which means "to unveil." In an apocalypse, the author reveals something to the knowledgeable reader through the use of symbolic numbers, colors, animals, and objects so that only believers could understand it.

This form of literature came into being during grave times of crisis. True believers were being persecuted for their faith, even to the point of martyrdom. The symbols, which predict the downfall of the oppressors, helped hide the message from the oppressors. At the same time, the inner circle (the true believers) knew how to decipher the meaning.

Apocalypses were written when the world seemed wholly lost, but their true meaning was that God would come soon and renew the face of the earth. Thus, an apocalypse has both a pessimistic and optimistic tone. Apocalypses give hope and consolation to a persecuted people.

Here are some other characteristics of apocalypses:

- The author usually chooses a pseudonym, often a holy or heroic figure from history;
- The viewpoint is cosmic. The whole universe is involved in the conflict. On the day of judgment, God will do the

202 DISCOVERING THE PROMISE OF THE OLD TESTAMENT

fighting; only a heavenly victory can win the battle. The apocalyptic event is not something human beings can bring about. God is in control and supernatural beings will fight the final battle.

■ Until that final day, the Day of the Lord, arrives, people must remain faithful, pray, and patiently await the Lord's arrival.

■ The just will one day rise from the dead. Their sacrifice will receive its reward. In fact, Dn 12:1–4 is the first place in the Hebrew scriptures that affirms a *personal* resurrection.

> "Of those who are sleeping in the Land of Dust, many will awaken, some to everlasting life, some to shame and everlasting disgrace. Those who are wise will shine as brightly as the expanse of the heavens, and those who have instructed many in uprightness, as bright as stars for all eternity" (Dn 12:2–3).

Looking to a New Era

The history of the Maccabees, Antiochus IV, the Hasmonean dynasty, and the Roman conquest brings the story of God's people down to New Testament times. As the first century B.C. came to a close, various Jewish religious groups, as well as the ordinary people, were still searching for a Messiah. Some lived a strict life in the desert, hoping that God's reign would come soon. Some preached the need to keep every precept of the Law before God would return to the people and set up a theocracy. Others abandoned Jewish traditions and looked to the culture of the Greeks and Romans for a new way to live. Still others believed in political compromise with the ruling powers to keep whatever privilege they still had. Some extreme groups advocated a violent overthrow of the Romans. But amid these various conflicting voices, God's word still spoke to the people.

Christians believe that the Hebrew scriptures find their completion in Jesus Christ. The messianic promises were fulfilled when God's own Son came to live among us as a humble carpenter. This simple man embarked on a teaching and healing ministry among the people. In his words and life he revealed God's word to us and is himself God's own Word who enfleshed the promises of the old covenant.

■ *research* ■

Read Daniel 7:1–28. List at least six images you identify as symbols.

Through vivid images, Daniel teaches a fundamental truth: the almighty God will defeat the forces of evil, the pagan rulers who are oppressing God's people.

■ *journal* ■

Check a good commentary (for example, *The New Jerome Biblical Commentary*) on Daniel 7. Find the meaning of the symbols you identified in your research assignment. Note them in your journal.

Of all the titles Jesus uses in the gospels to refer to himself, he uses the title "Son of Man" most often. The title refers in a generic way to "man," a human being. It also refers to the figure of Daniel 7:14 who will usher in God's kingdom. Scholars believe Jesus used the term in a paradoxical way to show that he was God's humble messenger of God's powerful kingdom.

Christians believe that Jesus' life, death, resurrection, and glorification complete the covenants God made with his people. We believe that Jesus is indeed the promised Messiah, the ideal son of David promised by the prophets. We believe that he is the Son of Man who has ushered in God's reign. We see him as the fulfillment of the promise made to Abraham that all nations would be blessed. The new covenant established in Jesus is for all people, in all places, for all times.

Christians have much to learn by reading, studying, reflecting on, and living the Hebrew scriptures. Without them we can never properly understand or appreciate what God has accomplished for us through Jesus. We owe much to our Jewish ancestors in the faith.

> And all these things which were written so long ago were written so that we, learning perseverance and the encouragement which the scriptures give, should have hope.
>
> — Romans 15:4

▪ *focus questions* ▪

1. Discuss two lessons the book of Tobit teaches.
2. How did Judith save her people? What important lesson does the book of Judith teach about God?
3. How does Judith represent the Jewish people? What does she tell us about Jewish women?
4. Identify Mordecai in the story of Esther. How did Esther save her people? What lesson does the book of Esther teach?
5. What is the feast of Purim?
6. Describe Jewish life under the Persian dynasty. Discuss two beliefs the Jews "borrowed" from the Persians.
7. Identify the term *Hellenism*. What was the goal of Alexander the Great?
8. Describe Jewish life under the Ptolemies.
9. Who were the Seleucids? Identify Antiochus IV. What were some crimes he committed against the Jewish people?
10. What was the "abomination of desolation"?
11. Who were the Maccabees? What did they accomplish for the Jewish nation?
12. What is the feast of Hanukkah?
13. What was the Hasmonean dynasty? What eventually happened to it? Identify Herod the Great.
14. Name three Maccabean leaders who figure prominently in 1 Maccabees.

15. Discuss several important theological themes that appear in 2 Maccabees.

16. Why did the tales about Daniel in the book named after him inspire the Jews?

17. When was the book of Daniel written?

18. What is *apocalyptic writing*? Discuss four characteristics of this literary form.

19. Why are the Hebrew scriptures vitally important to Christians?

■ *exercise* ■

Assume the role of the author of Daniel. Write a modern-day apocalypse to encourage Christians who are being ridiculed for their faith. Using symbols, compose a word picture that describes a Day of the Lord when all creation will recognize the goodness and activity of God in the world. Be prepared to explain your symbolism. (The essay should be 300–500 words in length.)

■

Prayer Reflection

We will end our study of the Old Testament with some stirring words of praise for our gracious God. These selections come from the book of Daniel.

> *May you be blessed, Lord, God of our ancestors,*
> *be praised and extolled for ever.*
> *Blessed be your glorious and holy name,*
> *praised and extolled for ever.*
> *Bless the Lord, all the Lord's creation:*
> *praise and glorify him for ever!*
> *Bless the Lord, all the human race:*
> *praise and glorify him for ever!*
> *Give thanks to the Lord, for he is good,*
> *for his love is everlasting.*

— Daniel 3:52, 57, 82, 89

■ *reflection* ■

Think of several people, talents, created goods, events in your life, and natural beauties for which you are grateful. Try to list twenty-five.

◾ *resolution* ◾

For the next week, praise and thank God for everyone and everything on your list. Put yourself in the Lord's presence, review the list, and praise the Lord for what the divine goodness has showered on you.

Glossary of Selected Terms

Allegory — A literary form that contains an extended comparison in which objects or persons stand for some other reality.

Anthropomorphism — A literary device in which human emotional qualities (e.g., sadness, anger) and physical traits (e.g., eyes) are attributed to God.

Aphorism — A short, easy-to-remember saying. The book of Proverbs contains many aphorisms.

Apocalypse — A Greek word for "revelation." It refers to a type of highly symbolic literature used to give hope to a persecuted people that God's goodness will triumph over evil.

Apocryphal books — From the Greek meaning "hidden," this word has two meanings. For Catholics, it refers to pious literature related to the Bible but not included in the canon of the Bible. Two examples from Old Testament times are 1 Esdras and the book of Jubilees. Protestants use this term to refer to several Old Testament books that Catholics consider inspired — Sirach, Wisdom, Baruch, 1 and 2 Maccabees, Tobit, and Judith. These books were not part of the Jewish canon of the Hebrew scriptures at the end of the first century, although they were found in Greek translations of the Old Testament. Catholics refer to this same list of books as "deuterocanonical."

Archaeology — In general terms, the study of antiquity. Technically, archaeology is the study of the material remains of past civilizations. It draws on many branches of learning and has contributed immensely to our understanding of the biblical world.

Canon (of the Bible) — The official list of the inspired books of the Bible. Catholics list forty-six books from the Hebrew scriptures and twenty-seven New Testament books.

Concordance — A book or computer program that contains key words of the Bible giving their citation by book, chapter, and verse.

Covenant — An open-ended contract of love God makes with people. The Old Testament tells us of some important covenants God made with the Chosen People, for example, the covenant with Abraham to bless him with descendants and the Sinai covenant with Moses to give the people a land and bless them as a nation. Biblical covenants require response on the part of the Israelites, especially living the Law. Christians believe that Yahweh made a perfect covenant with all people everywhere for all time in the person of Jesus Christ.

Dead Sea Scrolls — Discovered in 1947 in caves near the Dead Sea, these manuscripts belonged to the Jewish Essene sect that lived in a monastery at Qumran. The scrolls contain Essene religious documents, commentaries on certain Hebrew scriptures, and ancient Old Testament manuscripts. They have proved very valuable to scholars in studying the Old Testament and for learning about some Jewish practices at the time of Jesus.

Deuterocanonical — Greek word for "second canon." Refers to those books in the Catholic Old Testament that were not in the Hebrew canon but were in the Septuagint (Greek translation of the Bible) used by the early Christians. Catholics consider these books inspired while Protestants and Jews refer to them as apocryphal. These books are Sirach, Wisdom, Baruch, 1 and 2 Maccabees, Tobit, Judith, and certain additions to Esther and Daniel.

Deuteronomist — One of the primary sources of the Pentateuch, and particularly the book of Deuteronomy (designated "D"). This term also designates the author of Joshua, Judges, 1 and 2 Samuel, and 1 and 2 Kings. These works give a history of Israel from the time of the conquest until the Babylonian Captivity. The book of Deuteronomy serves as a kind of introduction to this history, one marked by an emphasis on covenant and reward for fidelity or punishment for infidelity.

El — A common Semitic word for God.

Elohist — A term used to refer to one of the major sources of the Pentateuch (designated "E"). The author used the Hebrew word *Elohim* to refer to God rather than the name *Yahweh* which was used by the Yahwist.

Essenes — A Jewish sect from the middle of the second century B.C. until the time of the Roman Revolt in A.D. 66–70. Their name means "pious ones," and they attempted to live a pure life of strict observance of the Law. Many of them lived in a desert monastery at Qumran near the Dead Sea. Scholars attribute the Dead Sea scrolls to them.

Etiology — A story that tries to explain the cause of a name, a practice, a custom, or the like.

Folklore — Beliefs, traditions, practices, and legends transmitted orally, often in story form.

Hanukkah — The Jewish Feast of Dedication which celebrates the recovery and purification of the Temple from the Syrians in 165 B.C. It is an eight-day feast that takes place during December near the Christian feast of Christmas. Also known as the Feast of Lights, Jews celebrate Hanukkah with gift-giving.

Hasmonean Dynasty — The Jewish kings descended from the Maccabees. They ruled from 135 B.C. to 63 B.C. when the Roman general Pompey conquered Israel.

Hellenism — The diffusion of Greek culture throughout the Mediterranean world after the conquests of Alexander the Great.

Herem — A Hebrew word that refers to the Israelite practice of sacrificing all booty and captives to God after a holy war.

Historical-critical method — This method of studying biblical texts tries to discover what the particular passage or book meant to its original audience.

Holocaust — A burnt offering in adoration to God in which the sacrifice was entirely consumed by fire. "The Holocaust" refers to the attempt by Adolf Hitler and his collaborators to annihilate the Jewish people in Europe during 1938–1945. It led to the destruction of over six million Jews.

Inspiration (of the Bible) — The guidance of the Holy Spirit that enabled the biblical writers to record what God wanted revealed.

Levites — Descended from Levi, one of the twelve tribes of Israel, Levites were entrusted with Israel's worship. They lived off the Temple offerings and owned no land.

Myth — A story that imaginatively expresses basic beliefs of a culture in narrative form. Myths often attempt to explain the origins of the world. The biblical myths particularly express belief in only one God who is good and who created a universe that is also fundamentally good.

Oracle — A message of God, usually in response to an inquiry. Old Testament oracles are delivered to prophets and priests. Many of the prophetic books contain oracles in poetic form.

Parallelism — A literary device that involves repetition and correspondence.

Passover — The most important Jewish feast; it celebrates the Exodus, Yahweh's deliverance of the Chosen People from Egypt.

Patriarch — Male ruler, elder, or leader. The patriarchs of the faith of Israel are Abraham, Isaac, and Jacob.

Pentateuch — A Greek word meaning "five scrolls." Used to refer to the first five books of the Bible — Genesis, Exodus, Leviticus, Numbers, and Deuteronomy. The books contain the Jewish Law, the Torah.

Pentecost — The Jewish feast of Pentecost, a harvest festival, occurred fifty days after Passover and celebrated Yahweh's giving of the Law to Moses. The Christian feast of Pentecost commemorates the descent of the Holy Spirit on the Apostles which occurred during the Jewish feast. Many gifts were poured out on the church at Pentecost.

Personification — A literary device that assigns human qualities to an inanimate object or abstraction.

Pharisees — An influential Jewish sect at the time of Jesus that put great emphasis on the observance of the Mosaic Law and oral interpretation of the Law. They believed in angels, bodily resurrection, and eternal life. They influenced the development of the synagogue. Their name means "separate ones." According to the Jewish historian Josephus, they first appeared during the reign of John Hyrancus (135–104 B.C.).

Priestly source — The name given to one of the author(s) of the Pentateuch (designated "P"). This source originated from priests who were in Exile. It gave final shape to the books of Genesis through Numbers and shows an interest in ritual rules and regulations, and legal and genealogical information.

Prophet — From the Greek, meaning "one who speaks before others." God entrusted the Hebrew prophets with delivering the divine message to rulers and the people. Most of them were unpopular in their own day. Most of their prophecies were written only at a later time.

Proverb — A short, memorable, popular saying that embodies traditional wisdom.

Sadducees — One of the leading groups in Judaism which held ruling authority from the time of the Hasmonean dynasty until the destruction of the Jewish Temple in A.D. 70. They were priests who traced their ancestry to Zadok, a high priest under King David. They were doctrinally conservative, rejecting beliefs such as the resurrection of the body. They only accepted the Pentateuch as inspired. But they were politically liberal — cooperating with foreign rulers such as the Romans and being influenced by Hellenism.

Samaritans — Descendants of the survivors of the northern kingdom left behind by the Assyrians. They intermarried with immigrants whom the Assyrians sent to Israel. They resisted the restoration of Judah during the time of Nehemiah and Ezra, worshiped Yahweh on Mount Gerizim, and became alienated from the Jews who thought of them as heretics and schismatics. They lived in the district of Samaria between Galilee in the north and Judea in the south.

Septuagint — An important ancient Greek translation of the Hebrew scriptures. The word "Septuagint" comes from the Latin word for "seventy" referring to the legendary 70 (or 72) scholars who translated the work in 72 days.

Tabernacles, Feast of — A Jewish harvest feast that takes place in our month of October and celebrates the harvest from the threshing floor and wine presses. It also goes by the name *Booths* or *Sukkoth*. It gets its name from the requirement to dwell in "booths" (tents) to recall God's protection of Israel during the wanderings in the desert.

Theophany — An appearance or manifestation of God, for example, when God "appeared" to Moses in a burning bush.

Torah — The Law handed down to the Jewish people which they were to live in response to God's covenant with them. A good summary of the Torah is found in the Ten Commandments.

Vulgate — St. Jerome's fifth-century (A.D.) translation of the Bible into Latin, the common language of the people of his day.

Yahweh — The sacred Hebrew name for God — YHWH — which means "I am who am" or "I cause to happen." Because the name was too holy to say aloud, the word *Lord* (*Adonai* in the Hebrew) was substituted whenever the sacred texts were read aloud.

Yahwist — The name given to the earliest literary source of the Pentateuch (designated "J"). The author(s) used the name *Yahweh* when referring to God, in contrast to the Elohist ("E") who used *Elohim* to refer to God. The Yahwist also employed anthropomorphisms.

Yom Kippur — The Jewish "Day of Atonement," a time of fasting and repentance, to make up for the sins of the past year.

Index